SLEIGHT OF MIND

How to Create and Experience Magic in Your Life

Rodrigo Diaz

10-10-10
Publishing

Sleight of Mind – How to Create and Experience Magic in Your Life
Diaz, Rodrigo
www.sleightofmindbook.com

Copyright © 2019 Rodrigo Diaz

ISBN: 978-1-77277-312-5

Publisher
10-10-10 Publishing
Markham, ON   Canada

Printed in Canada and the United States of America

Contents

I dedicate this book to every person looking for *that* answer; your journey is perfect and unique. Know that everything is possible; magic is real. Know that you have everything working in your favour to figure it all out. Thank you for sharing your magic with this world.

I also dedicate this book to Allison.
Every moment I share with you is a reminder that what's in this book is real—miracles exist.

And, of course, I dedicate this book to my mom and dad. Thank you for teaching me to see that magic is real.

Foreword

The book you are about to read is real magic.

As you already know, life is quite a journey; but if you are like most people, you are looking for one thing – peace. You are looking for a bigger understanding of how to be that powerful person you want to be.

No matter where you are in your personal journey, you are always where you need to be.

If you are interested in discovering the incredible power that you already have to create and experience miracles in your life, then you have found the right book. Author Rodrigo Diaz will take you on a fascinating journey to awaken and reconnect with that incredible, unique and unlimited energy within you.

Rodrigo intends to help you realize the magic within you; it is already there, you just need to remember how to use it. Through some wonderful eye-openers, Rodrigo spreads this message of love, understanding and self-empowerment.

Get ready to unveil the secrets to your true magic… Get ready to live your life from the best version of you!

Raymond Aaron
New York Times Bestselling Author

Acknowledgements

I want to thank my wife. Thank you, **Allison,** for believing in me, for always supporting me, for always being right next to me. Thank you for seeing the person I truly am. Thank you for sharing your life experience with me. You are so inspiring, strong, and kind. Thank you for making me live the experience of love. Thank you for being part of my love-manifestation dream. Thank you for being pure magic in my life. Thank you for making me feel real magic every day. **When I see you, I see the whole Universe. I love you. Te amo.**

I want to thank my mom, **Perla**, for being a true example of what our minds can achieve, and what miracles look like. Thank you for showing me, through your life example, that thoughts become things. Thank you for helping me become the man I am today. I am very fortunate to have you in my life. Thank you for all the love you share with me. I admire your passion for life and for learning. Thank you for my life, Mom. Gracias por siempre bailar conmigo y disfrutar de la vida.

I want to thank my dad, **Alejandro**. Thank you for being the greatest teacher of patience and love. Thank you for always seeing in me the power I talk about in this book. Thank you for being my best friend; thank you for being pure love. Thank you for everything you gave me and everything you didn't. I've always admired your positivity and kindness. You are my hero. Gracias por ser luz en mi vida.

I want to thank my sister, **Alejandra**. Thank you for growing up with me. Thank you for being in Canada with me. Thank you for sharing the experience of family with me. I couldn't have done half of the things I do if it weren't for you. Thank you for always helping me to get out of my comfort zone. Thank you for being weird and interesting. Thank you for showing me different levels of understanding. Thank you for being brave and moving to Canada so that I could see your example and follow it. I wouldn't be here if it weren't for you. Thank you for being you. Thank you for being one with me. Gracias por existir.

I am extremely grateful to have **Omar** in my life. Thank you for showing me what love and bravery can accomplish in this life. Thank you for all the time, advice, and love you share with me. Thank you for showing me how true change starts within. I admire you so much, Omar; and I love you so much. Gracias por ser puro amor.

To my **Quantum friends**, for all the times we reinvented reality and created time within time. Thank you for letting me talk to you about what creates magic in my life. Thank you for creating miracles with me. I am who I am today because of all those moments you provided your smile, your eyes, and your ears. I am extremely grateful to have found in you the reflection of the Universe. Thank you for sharing yourselves with me. I am blessed with your time as friends. Thank you; you have changed my life.

To my best friends, **Milan**, **Victor**, and **Jorge**. Thank you for showing me how our friendship goes beyond worlds. Thank you for all the lessons you keep showing me, even when you don't think you are. Thank you for seeing all my tricks. Thank you for sharing your magic with me.

I would like to thank **James**. Thank you, James, for being an incredible mentor. Watching you, listening to you, and being around you has been a very important part of all of what I am doing. This world needs more of your message of love. I can now see that the way we met was pure magic. Thank you for being an incredible inspiration and, most importantly, thank you for opening your heart to me.

Also, I would like to thank **Sathish**. Thank you for all the guidance and the incredible moments where you pointed me in the right direction. Thank you for listening and being honest when I needed it. You are an incredible example to me of what is possible.

I would like to thank **Richard**, my teacher, mentor, and friend. Thank you, Richard, for seeing the magic in me. Thank you for always having your door open. Thank you, because you keep teaching all kinds of different lessons.

Chapter 1
Sleight of Mind

The Set Up

The person that is writing this book right now, did not exist a year and a half ago. I was not *this version* of me. I was 32 years old, and I had a great job, a beautiful home, a wife, etc., but I felt sad, depressed, and incomplete. I felt stuck, and I felt trapped. I felt like things had no meaning. I couldn't tell you when it happened, but it felt like *this* had been happening for about five years now. I had jumped out of the driver's seat and into the passenger's side, and my life was just continuing without me. I felt like a zombie, crawling from one place to another, doing the same thing over and over again. Everything I was doing was being done on autopilot—my body didn't even need me anymore. It knew how to be sad, how to feel trapped, and how to live life without me enjoying it. I was letting my outer world create the reality in my inner world, even though I knew it should always be the other way around. I was waiting for something on the outside to change something on the inside, but that never came...

About three years ago, I had minor surgery. I should have taken that as a sign, but I didn't pay attention to it. A year and a half after that, my appendix exploded, and I had to be rushed to the hospital—sign number two. Three months after my appendix exploded, I was told that I had a small cyst in my thyroid—sign number three. A month later, I was told that I had disk herniation in my lower back. When this pain hits, it feels like a sharp knife in my lower back. When that happens, I am not able to stand for about two days, or go to the washroom, without help—or do anything for that matter—sign number... who knows by now; I've lost track of how many times the Universe was sending me messages through my body. Something needed to change. There were too many signs pointing out that something was wrong inside me. Life was telling me that I needed to stop the way I had been thinking, feeling, and behaving for the last few years of my life. Looking at it now, life was sending me messages of love so that I could wake up from my zombie state and take care of myself. Back then, it was hard to see, but something needed to change—me.

The Beginning

"There are only two ways to live your life.
One is as though nothing is a miracle.
The other is as though everything is a miracle."
– Albert Einstein

I've been practicing, studying, and performing magic (magic tricks) for about seven years now. At the beginning, it was a lot of fun being able to *fool* my friends with some simple tricks. Then, the more I got into magic, the more I understood the psychology behind it, and the more I realized that magic has nothing to do with fooling people. I understood that magic was all about creating and experiencing an impossible moment between two people.

As I evolved in the art of magic, I realized that magic is a shared experience; it's a gift. It's a piece of art that breaks the three-dimensional concept of reality, and creates the illusion of the fourth dimension (appearing and disappearing things, reading minds, etc.—again, it's the art of illusions). I started to see magic as an art form that creates feelings and emotions that take people back to feeling childlike wonder. Magic gives anyone a break from reality; it gives an experience of an impossibility.

Imagine experiencing a magic trick right now. Right after the end of the trick, for the first three to five seconds, you are in complete awe, in complete *"what-just-happened?"* (If the trick was performed well, of course.) Your brain is a little confused; it's enjoying a moment where the impossible just became possible. After those three to five seconds go by, your analytical part of the brain kicks in; it is now trying to figure out how the trick was done: "Where did the coin go?"

I've found that most people want to know the answer to the equation, as it is very hard to just let it go. But imagine taking those first three to five seconds when you were fully present and enjoying the impossible, and expanding that moment and that feeling of magic for a longer period of time. Imagine being able to live in this state of childlike wonder, knowing that magic is real, knowing that everything is possible, all the time. As a matter of fact, it is possible.

It was not until a couple of years ago that I started to see magic as something else, something powerful. The feeling I get when I see people's reactions to what's happening in front of them, is something hard to explain; it's quite magical. I wanted to create a way to make these feelings of happiness, wonder, and awe last more than just a few seconds. Perhaps there's a way to experience real magic and miracles in my life. Perhaps there is something in the idea that magic is real, and it is already part of who you and I are. This is where this project, *Sleight of Mind*, started.

I wrote this book, inspired by four things: my love for magic, my love for neuroscience (the understanding of how our brain works), my love for quantum physics (the deep study of the smallest particles of energy, its behaviour, and how we can relate to it), and my love for spirituality (an approach to knowing that we are all part of something bigger, that we are all here for a reason, that we are all one). These subjects have changed my life forever.

Magic

After almost eight years of practising and performing magic, I now give lectures on how to use principles of magic to create miracles in your life. For me, magic is the art of experiencing the impossible. The art of bending reality. The art of creating astonishment and a sense of wonder. For me, magic is a moment created by two people being fully present in one moment; it is a gift.

I've realized something special about magic that does not only apply to this art form, but it is the exact same formula for creating magic and miracles in your life:

1. **Magic happens in the unknown** – If you knew what was going to happen before the magic happened, you wouldn't feel the element of surprise. You wouldn't feel magic.

2. **Magic happens in the present moment** – If you miss the exact moment where the magic happened, it is quite hard to recreate that moment again. You have to be present in order to experience the trick, and real magic (miracles).

3. **Magic doesn't happen in my hands; it happens in your mind** – I know where the trick is; I know how it's done. I am simply presenting you with the right environment for your mind to create the magic. You are the one experiencing magic, not me. Magic happens in your head. You are the one creating it.

Neuroscience

Our brains are fascinating. I have a passion for understanding how our brain works and the powerful tool it is. It is incredible to me to analyze how thoughts become things. It is fascinating how our imagination can create any reality. It is quite magical to learn how imagination is more than just pictures in your head. It is very empowering to have the awareness and understanding that we can control what we think, feel, and do; yet we choose not to. It is deeply humbling to study the subject of habits. The deeper I've gotten into understanding what a habit is and how it is created, it is extremely interesting to realize that even you and I are a habit—but don't worry, we are going to get quite deep into all of this.

One thing is for sure, if you are committed to making a change in your life, understanding how your brain works is key to manifesting anything you want into your life experience.

Quantum Physics

It is quite an interesting subject. Sometimes it is hard to understand; sometimes it is simple to understand. I love studying the science that explains that everything in this Universe is energy. On the most basic level of Albert Einstein's E=mc2, the equation says that **energy** and **mass** (matter) **are interchangeable**; they are different **forms** of the **same thing**. Under the right conditions, **energy** can become **mass**, and vice versa.

This means that energy and matter are actually the same. This is an amazing eye-opener.

Everything in this Universe is energy. You and I are energy, our thoughts are energy, our emotions are energy, nature is energy, money is energy, etc. I've been reading and studying how energy affects matter (because matter is energy). I've been understanding how energy can never be created or destroyed— it can only be transformed—and that everything is connected. I've been understanding how everything is in constant expansion. I've been studying and reading how the energy of our thoughts and feelings affects our bodies for sickness and/or health.

I've been reading about this place called the Quantum Field, where everything and anything anyone could imagine or experience already exists, a place full of endless possibilities that you and I can always tap into. I've been studying how you and I can bring any experience into our lives through the energy of our thoughts and feelings: manifestation. I've been studying and practicing how thoughts become things, and how our imagination is the answer to all of this. Quantum physics is fascinating.

Spirituality

There has been a lot of misconception around this word. But the truth is that spirituality has nothing to do with religion. I didn't know this before, and once I understood this, a lot of the answers I was looking for, started to appear in my life. Understanding the fact that our inside world can create an effect on our outside world has been an incredible eye-opener in my life. It has been very humbling to understand that I am not a human that has energy inside, but that I am energy having a human experience. It has been confusing and liberating to study that I am not who I think I am—one of the most challenging concepts I've ever had, and continue to deal with. But through a lot of understanding and patience of who I truly am, I've been able to find peace, and I've been able to regain my true power, my true creative state of being.

These are the topics I talk about in my lectures, coaching sessions, and speaking gigs. I share information, experiences, and exercises on how to create and experience magic in your life.

I am by no means an expert on any of these four subjects. These are all passions of mine that I've been researching, studying, learning about, and practicing. I'm still trying to figure all of this out. I am on my own personal journey of finding my answers. I sometimes feel like perhaps I'm not the right person to share all of this, but please know that all of what you are about to read comes from a place of love. All of this comes from a place of knowing that inside of you, there is something that is always looking for happiness, love, peace, and joy. All I can do is share with you and show you the magic I see in you, and the magic I see in each one of these four subjects.

My honest opinion is that my knowledge on these subjects is like a grain of sand in the entire beach. There is so much to learn in this Universe; I am convinced that we, as humanity, know so little about what is out there. It is quite exciting to keep discovering the truths of the Universe.

I want to be open and honest with you. I want to share that I had felt afraid of writing about these topics, as not everyone wants to dive into them. But seeing the incredible changes that I and everyone around me is experiencing (family, friends, and other people), I am confident and inspired to share my journey with you. Now, more than ever, I'm convinced that the message is there if you want to listen to it. I am convinced that everything is connected. I am convinced that a miracle is just a decision away.

For me, magic ties it all together. I've been practicing all these three subjects, and when you put them all together, magic happens, and miracles simply happen. I've been able to experience changes in my life. I've been able to experience things manifesting into my life experience. I can see things that I wasn't able to see before. It has been quite a magical experience to play with all of these concepts. It has been quite interesting to discover what's behind the curtain. It is my hope that you also want to see what's behind the curtain. It is my hope that you, too, want to discover a new you. I hope you want to experience what real magic feels like.

Sleight of Mind is inspired by the teachings of all those wonderful masters this world has had, and keeps on having. Teachers, nowadays, come in any shape and form. They are regular people, just like you and I, and their message is full of love; they are teachers, doctors, scientists, comedians, actors, writers, and authors—people all around the world, spreading the same message of love, energy, and awareness. Thank you to all the ones I've had the gift and privilege to run into, study their work, and learn from their message: Dr. Joe Dispenza, Dr. Bruce Lipton, Francisco Alarcon, Dr. Wayne Dyer, James MacNeil, Gregg Braden, Neville Goddard, Alan Watts, Jim Carey, Albert Einstein, amongst many others.

Throughout this book, you will find yourself reading what appears to be similar or perhaps repetitive topics. It is all done with the intention to reinforce the experience you're about to go through. It is all with the intention to help you remember what was previously spoken about; it all ties in together. It is quite magical to see how neuroscience, quantum physics, and spirituality all tie in together somehow—that is magic.

I hope that in this book, you'll find something you haven't thought of or encountered before. Maybe you will find something that might challenge some of the current beliefs you have—beliefs that might have been preventing you from seeing things differently, or might have been stopping you from creating the magic you want to experience in your life.

My only purpose is to share how I've found a new way of thinking; a way that has helped me improve the way I live my life. And even though I've not yet mastered all of these concepts, I've experienced significant changes in my life and the people around me. These changes have truly made me believe in the power that I have to create what I want in my life. These concepts have helped me trust and strengthen the innate ability that you and I have to use our thoughts and feelings to create magic in our lives. All I ask from you is to be open to hearing a different perspective. Open your mind and heart to something new. Magic is a decision away.

Sleight of Mind

In order to explain what *sleight of mind* is, I have to explain what *sleight of hand* is.

While studying and performing magic, I fell in love with the idea of feeling childlike wonder again, feeling like anything can happen, and experiencing the impossible. For some reason, I wanted to share this feeling with others. I wanted to make people feel awe and wonder again. I wanted to remind everyone of how something so simple can be so incredible.

As a magician, I am able to manipulate cards, or any other small object, using hand coordination and finger dexterity. This happens without anyone else noticing, and it happens right in front of you. Such mastery of the hands (along with other principles that I will talk about in this book) helps create that experience of magic from your point of view. This is called *sleight of hand*.

Sleight of mind is the art of mastering **your mind**. *Sleight of mind* is **your** innate ability to use your awareness and consciousness through your thoughts and feelings, to create and experience magic in your life.

The "mind" is your brain and your heart in action, which are activated when you are practicing awareness and consciousness. Shockingly, these are *not active* most of the time. I will later explain how to activate them, and why, right now, they are most likely not being engaged.

Did you know that you live approximately 95% of your day on autopilot? Did you know that your daily life is being executed by a computer program (your habits), and that this program has turned you into a zombie, going from place to place, doing the same thing you did yesterday, and that you will probably do tomorrow? (Yes, this is probably happening to you, even though right now you might be thinking, "That's not me!") Don't worry; I will explain all of this in Chapter 2 – Illusions.

Imagine being able to control what you think and what you feel, all the time independently from any of the circumstances of your surroundings. Imagine being able to focus your thoughts and feelings to always live in your natural state of being: love, happiness, peace, and joy. Imagine living life knowing that you are unlimited, whole, and in love with life. Imagine being able to think and feel, and most importantly, see and create magic in your life. If you can master your thoughts, you can master your feelings. Master your feelings, and you will master yourself. Master yourself, and you will start to experience miracles in your life. This is *sleight of mind*.

The "I" in Magic

Most magicians got into magic at an early age. They either saw a magician at a birthday party, or someone from their family, that weird funny uncle, showed them the couple of magic tricks he had up his sleeve, or someone gave them a magic kit as a birthday present. That was not my case. I actually got into magic at the age of 22. I had just finished watching a movie, *The Incredible Burt Wonderstone*. This movie is a sitcom where an old-school magician faces the reality that he is no longer on trend anymore. I loved it.

This movie reminded me that I've always liked magic; but more than my love for magic, it reminded me that I love the emotions and feelings that magic makes people feel. It seems very powerful to me to be able to give someone a moment they can't re-create, an impossible moment. This *special moment* feels like a beautiful gift. It feels like an impossible gift; a moment so special that it can only live in your memory and your imagination—an experience that can never be repeated. That's right; the feeling you get, in the exact moment you are experiencing a particular magic trick for the first time, could never be repeated or recreated. If you watch a trick done for the second time, your first reaction to it could never be felt again— you now know what's going to happen.

For me, magic is the gift of a moment designed just for you. I understand that when I am performing a magic trick for you, magic doesn't happen in my hands. Think about it: I know where the secret move is; I know how the trick works. Magic happens in your head. Magic only exists inside your understanding of what's happening in that very moment. All I have done is to create the environment in which you can see this miracle happen. Your brain is the only thing that's bending reality for you. Your perception of what's happening is creating that magic moment. That's a really cool gift.

The deeper I got into magic, the more I became fascinated with understanding why magic works and how magic tricks are designed. I discovered the incredible amount of craft and thinking that goes behind creating such wonderful experiences. I also started performing and showing magic to others, and this is quite an experience on its own; you learn a lot about yourself putting yourself out there. This is when I started to see magic as an art form, as a performance piece. I started to understand that there is so much more than just knowing the secret behind the trick. I started to understand that knowing how it's done is just 30% of the whole experience. It is actually the performance that makes the magic. It is what I say during the performance; it is the ability to relate and connect to others that makes magic. Without you, there is no "I" in magic.

After a while, I found myself experiencing magic through other people's eyes. I developed a connection to what others feel while I perform magic. This connection has helped me realize that magic is a gift, a gift that can only be experienced in the present moment. It is a personal moment shared between your awareness and my consciousness. It is a gift to you as much as it is a gift to me—a moment where something impossible simply becomes possible.

This idea of the impossible becoming possible made me ask myself if I could experience *magic moments* in every aspect of my life. This is where the idea of this book started.

Magic Happens

As I continue to do my speaking gigs, perform magic, and develop my coaching career, I've noticed that there are a few principles of psychology in this art form that are very interesting and powerful; principles that are based in human behaviour and how the brain works. As a magician, I use things like your perception, imagination, assumptions, body language, and your focused attention to create the experience of magic—which by the way, only happens in your head.

I've always been fascinated how a magician can do a *secret move* in plain sight, without anyone being able to see what is really happening. Most secret moves happen right in front of you, and when they are well performed, you'll never notice them.

When you are experiencing a magic trick, the only difference between you and me is knowledge: I know how the trick is done. So, I want to share with you one of the biggest lessons magic has taught me:

"When you look at something impossible, in any area of your life, it's not that you cannot do it; it's just that you don't know how... not yet, at least."

I simply know what the secret is; I know where and when the *secret move* happens. That's really it; that's magic. So, when you apply this concept to your life, it just means that if you think about something you truly desire, and if it looks impossible to obtain, it's not that you cannot do it; it's just that you don't know how… not yet, at least. And that can change.

On a more personal level, magic has helped me bring moments of joy and a sense of wonder to people. That, to me, is a gift in itself. It makes me feel so much joy and happiness to see adults remembering what it's like to be a kid again, to feel childlike wonder, to stop being *adults* for a moment. I love to see when people are in touch with the invisible part of them that *knows* that anything is possible. We all have one. It has always been there; it has never left. As kids, we used to know that *everything* was possible, but we let our poor habits, our egos, and our limited perceptions of reality create limiting beliefs in our lives, blinding us from the truth that in fact everything is possible. Magic, for a second, puts us back in touch with that true power of knowing.

The more I studied and performed magic, I couldn't help but think: "Maybe there is a way to create real magic in my life. Maybe childlike wonder is something I can experience all the time. Maybe there is a way to experience miracles in my life. If life is an illusion (don't worry; we will get really deep into this in Chapter 2 – Illusions), how can I create a better one? Could I use my perception of things, my imagination, my thoughts, and my feelings to create and experience magic in my life? The answer to all of this is, "Yes, it is possible."

I want to be clear about something. This is not a book about positive thinking, or a self-help book. This is not a book about happy thoughts. Trust me, I've tried thinking positively before, and I've always felt like I was missing part of that equation. If you have felt similarly before— asking yourself if there is more to just thinking positive thoughts—well… you're right; there is more to discover. This book is meant to be a tool to go beyond that point.

Miracles/Real Magic

I think it is very important to talk about miracles, what they are, and your relationship to them. Some people believe in them while others do not, and there are some who don't really care about them. I hope that you are able to be aware that everything in this life is a miracle. You and I were not taught to look at things through this Universal truth. Most people were not brought up understanding what miracles are, what they represent, and how to interact with them.

People who believe in miracles experience more miracles than those who do not believe in them. This is just a fact. And the only reason they experience more of them is because, by putting their attention and awareness to the possibility of something incredible happening in their lives, it simply happens. Remember, what you put your attention on, you will create more of the same.

This is going to be a recurring subject throughout the book, so I would love for you to get familiarized with it:

> *"Where you place your attention*
> *is where you place your energy."*
> **– Dr. Joe Dispenza**

As a human being, you use your energy within, through your attention. Whatever you choose to give your attention to, that particular person, object, activity, thing, or yourself has your energy. So, if you place your attention on complaining about the weather, the Universe will bring you more experiences to complain about, as you are placing your energy on complaining. On the contrary, if you place your attention on how lucky you are to be living this life, the Universe will bring you more experiences so that you can continue to feel lucky, as you are placing your attention on feeling prosperous.

Miracles appear to be unpredictable. This is because a miracle can only exist in the *unknown*. If you could predict what was going to happen, it wouldn't be a miracle. In order to create more miracles in your life, you must create some kind of empty space in your life for them to appear. You must create more *unknown* in your life. If you do not create that empty space, there is no way a miracle will come—there's no place it can fit. You must be open to not knowing what's going to happen next in your life. I invite you to stop trying to fill up your daily life with tasks, things to do, and schedules to follow. Create empty spaces for *the unknown* to exist in your life. Stop trying to know what's going to happen every single second of your day. It's OK not to know. Start paying attention to the fact that you are lucky, and that everything is always working out for you. Start telling yourself that you are the receiver of unexpected surprises in your life. Start telling yourself that you attract miracles into your life.

You might argue that miracles are just coincidences. Thank you for bringing that up. You are totally right; a miracle is a coincidence. If we deconstruct the word, *coincidence*, we can see that "co" means together, and "incident" means an event or occurrence that happens. So, if we put this together, a coincidence is the co-creation (two elements coming together) of an event that simply happens. In this case, the co-creators of this event are you (the invisible part of you that is connected to the Universe) and the Divine Intelligence (The Divine Energy in the Universe). So, you're right, a miracle is a coincidence (a co–creation) between you and the Universe; a co–creation between the inner part of you and the outer part of you.

You and I were never taught how to interact with miracles. You and I were told that miracles *may* only happen once in a blue moon, and most likely not to you. But right now is the time to change your relationship and your understanding of this subject. Right now is the time to start developing a close relationship with miracles and real magic. You are a miracle magnet. Start to see and experiencing miracles in your life. Start accepting that miracles happen. After all, if you take a close look at yourself, you are a miracle (I will explain this part of you being a miracle in Chapter 8 – Understanding Real Magic).

The Universe, this Divine Intelligence, talks to you through miracles—miracles is its language. And the most interesting part about this is that if you are not open to seeing and experiencing miracles in your life, they will simply pass you by, even though they might be right in front of you. They will try to grab your attention; they want you to notice them, and unless you are open to them and have the consciousness to receive them, you will not be able to recognize them. Recognizing miracles requires a level of consciousness and awareness that you need to unlock. It is a higher vibration that you need to experience and stay in. Just because you achieve this level of consciousness once, it doesn't mean that you will stay there forever; if you move your awareness from it, you can just as easily fall back into blindness. Miracle-awareness is a constant state of being that you must learn to live in.

A miracle is defined as a surprising, extraordinary event that is inexplicable by natural or scientific laws. What I would like you to take out of this is the understanding that a miracle is something out of the ordinary. This is the part where you must learn how **not** to live life in your past (which you are doing 95% of the time), and learn how to live life in the unexpected (you will read more on living in the past, in Chapter 3 – The Power of the Brain.)

I'm sure you've experienced some kind of miracles in your life. It could be anything from thinking of an old friend and having that friend contact you shortly after, to experiencing a very "lucky," unexpected moment of fortune, like finding money on the street, etc. What you didn't realize back then, which I hope you start to realize now, is that YES, it was a *coincidence*—a co-creation between the inner part of you and the Divine Energy that lives everywhere and in everything.

There is one more important detail to mention when understanding how miracles work: You cannot control the circumstances or conditions around a miracle. You cannot say *what, when,* or *how* a miracle will show up in your life experience. You cannot force a miracle to happen to you; you can only be open to receiving it—and trust me, you will receive it.

The way to attract a miracle into your life is by paying attention to the feelings you would feel if you were to obtain the "thing" you desire. You should also know that this miracle entering your life might not be exactly what you wanted. It might not be exactly what you thought it would be, but I promise that it would make you feel the same way you would feel if you had gotten the thing *you thought you wanted.* This miracle will make you feel the love, peace, joy, abundance, security, in-love-with-life, magical, empowered, luck you were looking for. And the reason for this is that you don't really want what you think you want. You must learn how to look beyond what you want. For example, you don't really want more money; you want to feel secure. You don't really want extra time in your day; you want to feel freedom. You don't really want to get rid of an addiction; you want to feel healthy, etc.

So, in order to allow a miracle into your life experience, you have to combine your intention (defining what you would like to experience, and the feelings related to that experience) with your attention (being aware of the thoughts and feelings related to that particular experience; in other words, how it feels to live life as if you already have what you desire). The rest is not up to you. Stay open minded. Look for the miracles—they are everywhere. Learn how to speak miracles. Learn to identify what real magic looks like. Build a relationship with this Love Force— the Universe. Remember:

"*Those who believe in miracles experience more of them.*"
– James MacNeil

A miracle is not a miracle unless it is recognized.

Chapter 2

Illusions

The Illusion of Life

You are not you. You are not who you think you are. You are not a physical body that has an energy-soul inside—you are not your name; you are not your age; you are not your identity; you are not your personality; you are not even a husband, a wife, a brother, a sister, a mom, a dad, an employee, or a friend—you are not who you think you are.

You are *you*. You are what you *feel* you are. You are a spiritual being in a physical form. You are placed into this life to experience happiness, love, peace, and joy. You are pure Divine Energy; you are part of it all, and you are connected to it all. You are everything you believe to be. You are part of the Divine Intelligence that created all life. You are a creator. You are unlimited. You are powerful. You are creative. You are greatness. You are love. You are compassion. You are part of the Infinite Energy that created all worlds—you can create your own world.

Your identity and personality are just thoughts that you keep repeating to yourself every day and every moment of your life. Every day when you wake up in the morning, consciously and subconsciously, you tell yourself that you have a certain name, that you belong to a certain city, that you belong to a certain group, that you are a certain age, that you have a certain job, that you have a family, that you are from a certain ethnicity, etc. Your whole personal reality is based on thoughts and information that were created in the past. All this information was either created in the past or it was passed on to you.

This information is just ideas that you have decided to believe and embrace as truths; you are deciding to repeat these ideas over and over again, every day. Imagine doing this for years. Imagine repeating certain information of what *you think you are*, like your name, gender, age, what you are capable and not capable of, etc., over and over again, without you being aware of what's happening. Without you knowing it, you are living inside a perfect illusion you have created for yourself. And it is all based on information and events that happened in the past. And the worst thing is that you might be so deeply emerged into these repetitive thoughts and patterns that right now your brain might be trying to argue that what I'm saying is wrong: "How could I not be myself?" Please, just be open to hearing this:

"You are a compilation of habitual thoughts, emotions, and behaviours that you have chosen to repeat over and over again."

The snowball of your repetitive thoughts, emotions, and behaviours got so big that it is almost unstoppable, and almost impossible to understand. You truly believe that you are your name, your age, your job title, your identity, and your personality. But you are not who you think you are. Remember, beliefs are just thoughts that you keep repeating to yourself.

Life as you know it is just an illusion. As humans, we have created a series of ideas that "helped" shape what we know as a society (I personally don't think these ideas helped too much). All of these ideas became what you now believe to be how the world is *supposed* to work: people going to work, having a job, paying taxes, *saving* for the future, buying marketed products, looking to retire, poor-middle-high classes, etc. But all of these concepts are just a series of thoughts and ideas that you and I kept repeating over and over again, and eventually we accepted them as truths; they became our beliefs. And most of the time, without knowing it, these ideas ended up creating limiting beliefs in our lives; beliefs that get in the way of you actually reaching your full potential. They are limiting beliefs that blind you and me from understanding who we truly are: a *powerful spiritual energy being*, living in physical form, capable of everything, and capable of creating and manifesting miracles in our lives.

You and I have chosen to blindly follow what others have repeated in their heads and lives for centuries. And it is almost never that you paused and tried to figure out the truth—the answers to why you are here in this Universe. Why now? Why not a hundred or a thousand years ago; or even why not ten years earlier?

You might have created a similar *illusion* to the one I just described above, without knowing it. I can assure you that you didn't mean to. You were just following a life pattern that has been passed on to you. You were taught to live in this *illusion*, where everything is a certain way, based on how everyone else has always lived their lives. You were taught to live in this *illusion* where you have to look for something on the outside to make you feel happy and whole on the inside (like buying a car, house, or new phone, or like getting a new job, or moving away from home, etc.). You were taught that only working hard and suffering long hours is the way to success: *"Success only comes with hard work."* You were taught that buying things, being busy, being stressed at work, paying for a mortgage, running from place to place, etc. is the way life is supposed to be. But it is all an illusion. None of this is true. You are not here to survive. You are here to create. You are here to experience love, happiness, peace, and joy. Everything else is just an illusion created by separation, by fear. Everything else is an idea created by human ego.

I hope that these last few pages have opened your mind to the possibility that perhaps there is something that you might not have been thinking about—something a little different from what you are used to. I will start to explain everything on a deeper level. But for now, thank you for being open to understanding that you were placed in this Universe to experience love, happiness, peace, and joy. Everything outside of that is not natural.

Remember this: What's normal these days (people feeling stress, anxiety, lack, anger towards each other, running in desperation because they are *late*, not enjoying life, etc.) is not *natural* (happiness, love, peace, and joy). And what's *natural* (feeling love, happiness, peace, love, and creating miracles in your life) is not normal (you don't see it quite often).

Survival Mode vs Creative Mode

Your body is an instrument of perfection. Inside of it, there is a natural flow of energy meant to be used in two very different ways: to survive and to create. This flow of energy moves through eight energy centres throughout your body. An energy centre is a very strong concentration of energy inside your body—you might know them as *chakras*. The first one is located behind your reproductive organs. The second one is behind your belly button; the third one is located at the top of your stomach: *your gut feeling*. The fourth one is inside your chest cavity, your heart, and this is the biggest energy centre you have. The fifth one is located in the middle of your throat. The sixth one is *your third eye*, in the middle of your eyebrows and behind your eyes. The seventh one is at the top of your head, inside the top part of your skull. And the last one, the eighth one, actually sits about a foot and a half above your head. This is the only energy centre that sits outside of you.

These energy centres are meant to help you create a perfect flow of energy throughout your body, but most people have their energy stuck in the first three centres. These three first centres have to do with your feelings. This is where your survival mode exists (feeling stressed, anxious, fearful, angry, sad, etc.). And if you cannot let the energy flow beyond this survival mode, it will never get past your first three energy centres, into the last five energy centres, where your creative mode exists.

Survival Mode

Let's go back in time to the prehistoric era. Picture a caveman. Now, imagine the moment when this caveman saw a giant T. Rex; at that exact moment, his survival mode kicked in. Seeing imminent danger activated his survival instinct of fight or flight. This fight or flight mode releases a chemical reaction known as adrenaline, along with feelings of anger, fear, stress, and anxiety, which are all meant to help this caveman fight or take flight. In this case, the caveman chooses to escape, and runs away as fast as he can. Once he is far from the danger, and the T. Rex is no longer in the picture, he is able to go back to living a peaceful life. He goes back into a natural state of being.

All animals and humans still have this survival mode as part of their nature; it helps us stay alive. Yes, there is no T. Rex running around eating people these days, but the interesting thing is that in today's world, you have created multiple T. Rexes—not in bone and flesh, but in thoughts. And the worst part is that for you, this *T. Rex* never goes away; you are always running away, and always fighting. You are living most of your life in survival mode.

Today's *T. Rex* has different shapes and forms. Your monster(s) appears in the shape of your job, the bills you have to pay, debt, work emails in the middle of the night, traffic, your routine, a family member you don't like, the memories of something that happened to you a couple of years ago, lack of money, the excessive amount of things to do, an acquaintance you don't like, something you saw in social media, the way someone reacted to something you posted on social media, that person that cut you off in traffic, something you heard in the news, etc.—you name it! This *T. Rex* can take a lot of different shapes and forms. But the interesting thing is that all day long, you are putting your attention (your energy) on every single one of these different shapes and forms. From the minute you wake up, to the second you go to bed, you are thinking about these T. Rexes. They never go away, causing you to release adrenaline, creating feelings of fear, stress, anxiety, and anger. These T. Rexes are so powerful that even when you are not physically in any of the situations mentioned above, you are still thinking about all of them. You think about them in your commute, in the shower, when you eat, and even when you're in bed. This is how you stay in survival mode all day long. This is how you're not able to let your energy go beyond your survival mode. Your T. Rex never goes away!

Don't worry, we will talk about how to get beyond survival mode later in the book. It is all a series of exercises that you will be reading about later on.

Creative Mode

Your creative mode starts in your heart, which I mentioned is the biggest energy centre you have. Your creation mode is your natural state of being. It is where happiness, love, peace, and joy are always present. From this state of being, you are able to create new experiences and manifest new things into your life: miracles. You must be able to get past your survival emotions, and tap into the creative emotions of happiness, love, joy, and peace in order to create what you want for your life experience.

As illustrated in the example above (the T. Rex), as long as you feel the emotions of fear, stress, anger, and anxiety, your mind will not be able to focus on creating; and how could it? When you are in survival mode, it is time to run away, it is time to defend yourself, it is time to escape. Try analyzing yourself. You might find out that 99% of the things you are paying attention to in your daily life are causing you some kind of survival emotions, which are stopping you from tapping into your creative mode.

In the following chapters, we will also get into how to tap into this creative mode, with exercises and more theory that will help you get more familiarized with all of these concepts. For now, I just wanted to share with you these two different modes of living, and the importance of being able to identify the difference between them. You want to be able to stay in your creative mode for as long as possible. Again, it is your natural state of being.

A simple way to start noticing which mode you are living in, is to be the observer of your life. Remember, your heart is the epicentre of all the amazing feelings you could possibly experience. You must train yourself to *think* with your heart. All the answers live there. If at any point in your life something troubles you, simply ask yourself, while focusing on that energy centre, "Will what I am about to do (think, or say) bring me peace? Or will it bring me turmoil? Always do, think, and say what brings you peace and joy.

The Illusion of Separation

You and I were taught to believe that everything is separate from us. You were taught that you are separate from me, and that what you desire in this physical world is separate from you. Even the way you were taught to speak is a program that creates more separation (I will explain this in the following paragraphs). And none of these is true—and understanding the truth is part of the manifestation process.

You and I are not separate. You are not separate from that person that cut you off while driving either. You are also not separate from everything that you desire. Because you have a body and I have a body, it might look like we are separate, but we are not. The energy that lives inside of you (what you are made of), also lives inside everyone and everything; yes, animals and objects too. Everything in this Universe is made out of energy. Everything is made out of this Divine Energy Force. It is everywhere—it is universal; it is in everything—otherwise it wouldn't be called universal. Therefore, when you understand that everything you desire is already in this physical world, when you understand that you and I are the same energy, you know that you are not separate from anything or anyone.

Think about it this way: It's as if I were trying to convince you that your pinky is separate from your thumb. Yes, looking at the *smaller picture*, it does look like your fingers are separate, but your thumb and your pinky are attached to your hand, which is attached to your arm, which is attached to your body. They are attached to something bigger, and they are still part of the same. The Energy Force, of which the Universe is made of, is your body; and you and I, and everything you desire, are the little fingers of this energy in the Universe.

Language can also reinforce this illusion of separation. Here are some of the words you use that create separation between you and your desires: "I want," "I wish," and "I hope." By saying those words, you are putting your desires in the future, and you are putting your desires outside of you. The future will never come to you—it lives in the future! By saying these words, you are acknowledging that right now, in this present moment, you do not have what you desire—you are not experiencing any of it. Even though you might feel happy when you "wish, want, or hope" for something, what you are really doing is putting your attention on the *lack of it*, instead of putting your attention on believing and feeling as if you already have it.

In the Spiritual Universe, there is not time; time is just an illusion created by man. You either are or you are not; there is no such thing as becoming (or obtaining). The moment you wish, hope, or say that you want something, you are creating separation from it. You are putting *it* somewhere in time where it's not right now; you are putting your desire somewhere in time where you will never experience it—tomorrow.

You are so hard on yourself when you don't have that wish that you have been working at for a long period of time. What you haven't realized is that you have been creating separation between you and your desire, with your words.

You must *be* your desire, to attract *that* into your life. You must be happy to attract more happiness; you must be love to attract love; you must feel and be abundant to attract more abundance. You must feel healthy (with your imagination and feelings) to attract health into your life. Even though your physical experience might be showing you something different, remember that your *physical world* is just an illusion. Your *outer world* is just a reflection of your *inner world*. Stop using "I want," "I wish," or "I hope," to talk about your desires.

There is no separation, only the illusion of it. We all come from the same place—energy—and we are all one. And even though it might not look like it—an illusion—everyone and everything is just an expression of love. If you are able to understand that all your desires are attached to you by energy (like the fingers in your hand), then what you desire has to come to you, as it is already here, it is already a part of you, and it already exists in this physical world. You really are just aligning yourself with it. Everything you desire is an extension of you.

We Are All One

I would love to share one of the best analogies I've ever heard about the understanding of how we are all one. Between one of the greatest metaphysics teachers this planet has ever had, Dr. Wayne Dyer, and my interpretation of his analogy of the ocean, my hope is to share with you the understanding and the love of the fact that *we are all one.*

Imagine an ocean, beautiful, powerful, and vast. If I dip a glass into that ocean, and I put that glass on a table, what's inside of that glass? The answer is *ocean water*; right? Now imagine I take a second glass, and I also dip this second glass into the ocean, and I put it on a different table. What's inside this second glass? The answer is also *ocean water*. Just because I put a glass on one table, and a different glass on another table, it doesn't mean that they contain different *water*. Both came from the ocean, and they are still *ocean water*. Now imagine I do the same thing with hundreds and hundreds of glasses, and I put them all over the place, on different tables; and perhaps a lot of them are sharing the same table. They are all still ocean water.

Now imagine that the ocean is not an ocean. Imagine that the ocean is Infinite Energy Source. Imagine that this ocean is the energy from which everything is made. Now imagine that all the glasses I was talking about before are not glasses. Imagine that all these "glasses" are all "cases of flesh." See where I'm going with this? You and I are the glasses, and what's inside of us is all the same—a part of Source. We are all part of this Divine Energy.

So, if we are the glasses, and this Divine Energy is the ocean, we are all part of the same Source. Not only did we all come from the same Source, but we are all still the same at our core—Source Love. Just because you came into this world in a "glass" that looks like you, it doesn't mean that you are any different from another "glass" that lives in a different country—or from another "glass" that cuts you off in traffic, or from another "glass" that doesn't share the same beliefs as you, or from another "glass" that doesn't look at life the way you do, etc. The invisible part of you and me is the same; we are all the same. We are all one with Source. We are all one.

I hope you are able to embrace this understanding. It is quite warming and, most importantly, it is true. After understanding something like this, how could you ever be angry or mean toward anybody else? How could you ever try to make someone else feel bad, even if it's by accident or non-intentional? You would always be aware of everything and everyone around you. All you would see in others is more of you. All you would see in others is yourself. All you would see in others is pure love. We are all one. Everyone around you is only reflecting what you have inside. A person (or his/her action) doesn't make you mad; what makes you mad is what you see in that person, which turns out to be just a reflection of something you might find limiting in yourself.

Being angry at someone else, trying to make others feel bad, pointing out someone else's mistakes, or being mean to others, etc., is redundant—you are doing it to yourself. This is why everything, from wars to insults, to arguments of who is right and who is wrong, etc., are all hurting this planet—we are all one. At our core, we are all the same. Physically and spiritually, we are all looking for one thing: inner peace. Every desire you have, every wish you would like to fulfil—anything, big or small—all you want at the end is to feel peace; and so does everyone else on this planet, including animals and nature.

When everyone in this world lives through the understanding that we are all one, love will be the one thing that unites us all. We will understand that the planet is also one with us. We will all finally understand that whatever we are doing to this planet, and the living creatures in it, we are consequentially doing it to ourselves. I truly believe that if we could all live with this thought and understanding of life, the world would be an even more kind, peaceful, and loving place. We should all live like the beautiful song, "Imagine," written by John Lennon.

> *"I hope someday you'll join us.*
> *And the world will live as one."*
> – John Lennon, "Imagine"

The Illusion of Time

> *"We are living in a culture entirely hypnotized*
> *by the illusion of time."*
> – Alan Watts

Time is just an illusion created by mankind. The truth is that there is no time. Life is just one eternal moment. Life is simply one moment that never stops. What matters is what is happening now, and now, and now, and now...

Time is an idea created by man to give some kind of *fake order* and *fake structure* to a controlled and limited way of living. Things like running late, being early, running out of time, etc. are ideas to reinforce your attachment to this illusion of time. You only have this present moment. Life is just one moment that keeps on happening. But somehow, it seems that mankind is a prisoner of time.

Time was created by a limited thought, a thought that originated from fear and a need of control. The present moment you are living in is all you have. This is why staying in the present moment, by using your awareness, is a practice you need to master. Don't give your energy away to the idea of time; don't get caught up on the past (which is already gone, and it doesn't exist), nor on the future (which will never come, and it doesn't exist). It will only make you feel scarcity, anxiety, fear, and stress. Meetings, appointments, age, schedules, running late, etc. are just illusions to control your life. These are all ideas that, yes, we all experience, as we live in a world that is not all on the same level of consciousness, but of which you don't have to be limited by anymore. It is your choice from now on to understand that your life is just one eternal moment that keeps on happening. Don't give in to this illusion of time.

There is no before, and no after. The past will never happen again; it never did. The future will never happen; it will never come. This is why you cannot put a goal in the future. The future will always be in the future. You have to live your dreams and desires right now; you cannot put them in the future. You have to be that person right now. You have to be happy, peaceful, healthy, wealthy, etc., right now. If you are not able to start, right now, living life from that highest version of yourself (the perfect version of you that is abundant, happy, loving, healthy, wealthy, etc.), you will never become that of which you keep placing inside an illusion that doesn't exist—the illusion of time. Imagination is not a tool that was gifted to you just by chance. Imagination is the tool given to you by Divine Intelligence so that you can live that life right now; as *right now* is the only time you truly have. You really can't become something; you simply have to be that something right now.

"As you think, you shall be."
– Bruce Lee

Think about the people who, throughout history, achieved greatness. It might have seemed like they started from nothing and eventually got everything they wanted. What really happened is that they got it all because from day one, from the beginning, they lived inside their heads; they lived their visions in their present lives, and they lived their lives from that highest place. Their visions in their minds were so strong and so clear that they were living in those lives before anything was even present in this physical world. They understood that in order to *get* something, you have to *be* that something. They understood that the time to *be* that something, was *right here and right now.*

"Yesterday is history, tomorrow is a mystery,
but today is a gift. That is why it is called the present."
– Master Oogway, Kung Fu Panda

The Illusion of Control

One of the hardest things to do in life is to learn how to simply let go. One of the hardest things to do is to not think about the thing you do not want to think about. It's very hard to let go of the need to control any outcome. It's all we were ever taught how to do. When parents tell their kids what to do, what not to say, and how to behave—control. When you try calling or texting that person that you really like, but she or he is not responding—control. When you feel the need to know how your day is going to unfold, the places you need to go, the things you have planned to eat, the schedule you have to follow—control. When you feel the need to do something about that other something that is bothering you—control. The illusion of control is one of the hardest ones to break, and it is everywhere.

The illusion of control can only be broken when you decide to go with the flow and to let go. Understanding how to go with the flow is simple yet complicated. If you are "late" to work because all of a sudden you are stuck behind a traffic jam, and/or the subway line is not working that particular morning, your illusion of control kicks in, making you feel anxious and stressed. You are experiencing the illusion that things are not working out for you, while the opposite is true. You are always where you need to be. You are always experiencing what is best for you.

Imagine being in a slow river. I'm sure you can imagine how relaxing it is to feel the water around you, and I'm sure you can imagine how smooth the journey down the river is. Are you able to apply that same feeling toward the circumstances that are happening around you in this present moment? If you are stuck in traffic, that experience is perfect for you right now. If the line up at the bank is huge, that experience is where you need to be right now. If the person right next to you on the train is loudly speaking over the phone while being in the quiet zone of the train, you are in the perfect place. Be at peace with what is, no matter what that is.

Control doesn't exist. Control is just fear. Control is just resistance that you are creating against the flow that holds everything together. Control is just your ego in action. Control is just a judgement of what you think of as right or wrong. The more you try to control, the less you truly achieve. Letting go is trusting that there is a Divine Intelligence keeping everything moving in perfect harmony, and that everything is moving at the right place and at the right time. Everything is always working out perfectly for you; just let it be. You are where you need to be.

Everything around you is perfect. The second you want to change someone's behaviour or the way something external is playing out, you are falling into the illusion of control. The only thing that you can truly change and control is *you*.

The Illusion of Attachment

I have previously spoken about the illusion that you are not really who you think you are, and that you are not your identity or your personality. The illusion of *you* creates a deeper illusion, called the illusion of attachment—the illusion of believing that you are defined by your materialistic possessions (which I will further explain, are not *yours*). This is how you get caught up in an eternal loop that keeps feeding itself—the illusion of your personality reinforces the illusion of attachment, and vice versa; the loop never ends.

Your house is not yours; your partner is not yours; your son and/or daughter is not yours; your happiness is not yours; your... Let me try to explain this one for you. There is no "mine" or "yours." Things simply are; things simply exist. Everything in this Universe is simply happening. The second you think from within the identity and the personality which you have blindly believed that you are, you are not able to be in the present moment, and you are not able to experience your true unlimited self—you will always create the illusion of attachment.

Here is an example that I hope illustrates the above: "Your" house is not "your" house; "my" house is not "my" house. The structure you call "your" house, and the structure I call "my" house, are simply the experience of *a house*. There is no such thing as "your" mom either (for example); this person you call "Mom" is simply another spiritual being helping your energy live the experience of love in the form of a family.

The same applies toward feelings. There is no such thing as "your" happiness and "my" happiness; there is simply the experience of happiness—happiness anyone can tune into. There is no such thing as "my" abundance and "your" abundance; there is simply the experience of abundance—abundance anyone can tune into. You either jump on the train of these experiences or you don't. Through all this baggage of having an identity, legal papers, birth certificates, and other circumstances, you have created the illusion that things are "yours," but there is no such thing as "*your* ___" or "my ____." Everything is simply an experience.

I want to be clear; I am not saying that I don't want you to experience everything and anything you desire in your life. I am simply saying that if you are able to detach yourself from the illusion of attachment, you will simply experience everything in a deeper and more meaningful way. This will only result in you being able to tune into higher potentials. If you are able to let go of "yours," "mine," "his," "hers," etc., you will realize that everything is already happening in this Universe, and every experience is already happening in this physical world right now. Happiness, love, health, wealth, abundance, freedom, peace, joy—everything is happening right now, and you can experience it when you don't make it "yours." You simply have to tune into the vibration of what you desire to experience right now.

This Universe is infinite; it can never end, as it has no beginning. This Universe is pure abundance; it is always full of infinite happiness, peace, joy, etc. All of these experiences are always happening. But the minute you bring a personality into the equation—the minute you bring words like "mine" and "yours" into the equation—you are creating separation. It is hard to experience something at its fullest when you start dividing it into parts. Things are simply happening always, and if you can get rid of the illusion of attachment, by letting go of your personality, you will create a sense of freedom; you will simply experience things for what they are—pure experiences that are already happening now.

The word, *personality*, comes from the word, *persona*, which in Greek means *mask*. This means that your personality is just a mask you are wearing. Your personality is not really the true you (an unlimited, powerful, all mighty, creative energy being). Are you able to see that everyone is just wearing a mask of who they think they are?

It's really hard for all of us to realize that we are not this illusion we think we are. It is hard for anyone to realize that we are pure Divine-Love-Energy that came into this human experience called life, to live and experience our hearts' desires. Unfortunately, through these illusions of attachments, control, separation, time, and personalities (our egos), we have forgotten how to live connected to Source; we have forgotten how to live connected to our true loving, powerful, and godlike nature.

Breaking the Illusion

Everything in this Universe is energy. The smallest particles that exist in this Universe are energy. Everything in this Universe is made out of energy. It is what nature is made of. It is what the oceans, stars, sun, animals, trees, mountains, rocks, etc. are made of. It is also what anything material is made of, such as money, cars, houses, etc. It is also what thoughts and feelings are made of. It is what you and I are made of. Our cells, and their smallest particles (the electrons), are made out of energy. It might look like we are matter, but we are simply energy moving really fast, creating the illusion of matter. I will not get deep into the science of this, but I hope you are aware that everything in this Universe is energy. Perhaps there is a reason why, toward the end of the day, we tend to say: "I am running out of energy."

There are two worlds we must be aware of: the Physical Universe and the Spiritual Universe. Please keep in mind that they are both part of the same universe, as the word, *universe*, means one, but to be able to explain each one of them, it is easier to separate them for now. Also, there are other names for the Spiritual Universe; you might have also heard names such as: Quantum Field, Invisible World, Source, Vortex, etc. They all refer to this higher power that created everything.

I would like you to think of the Spiritual Universe as "the cause," and the Physical Universe as "the effect." Most people try to change a situation or circumstance in their lives, from within the Physical Universe (which is not possible). They try to change matter with matter. But only energy can change matter. If you change your energy, you change your matter (your life).

So, if you would like to change anything in your current life, or create something completely new, you have to do it from within the Spiritual Universe. You have to do it from the place that is the source of all things and the source of all energy.

The laws of the Universe apply to you and me, whether we like it or not, and whether we are aware of it or not. This is why it is so important to take the time to create the awareness of all the thoughts and feelings that go through your head every second of every day. This is why it is so important to take the time to build a perfect version of yourself. This is why it is so important to get beyond your *survival mode,* and live from your *creative mode.*

Some of the questions you might be asking yourself right now may be: "How can I change that which has the illusion of being real (physical) from that place which seems not real (non-physical, energy)? Let's jump into the three most basic, yet most important actions you can take right now to start changing your life.

You cannot go into the Spiritual Universe with your body, your name, your age, your identity, your personality, etc. To get into the Spiritual Universe, you cannot "cross" to the other side as matter; you have to become pure energy. Later in the book, I will explain how to do all of this, through closing your eyes. But for now, there are three human actions that are able to exist in both the physical and the Spiritual Universes. These actions can go in and out of both universes, on command. You can do this at any time, and you should practice *these,* consciously every day. They are the key to ignite the change you want to see in your world. These are: what you **think**, what you **write**, and what you **say**.

Interestingly enough, these three actions are true forms of manifestation. Let's do a quick exercise that will explain why what you **think, write, and say** are not only true forms of manifestation but are also the tools you need to master to help you in your manifestation process...

What you write

On a blank piece of paper, write down something you truly desire, anything you want (write it in the present tense, as if you already have it). Maybe start your sentence like this: "I am so happy and grateful now that (insert your desire here) ..." Now that you have finished writing your sentence, take a step back and look at the sheet of paper; take it in... and let me explain to you what just happened: true manifestation.

Before you wrote something on that piece of paper, there was nothing. And from nothing, it became something. When I first asked you to write a desire of yours on a sheet of paper, you first had to create silence inside your head, and you then focused your thoughts. You then *grabbed* a thought, which was floating somewhere in the Spiritual Universe (as all thoughts that anyone could have, already exist in the Spiritual Universe), you took your pen, and through an inspired action, you moved your hand across the paper and wrote that desire. A few moments ago, this piece of paper had nothing on it. You manifested a thought in the form of a sentence that started as nothing. And now, this thought is fully formed in this physical world, which seconds ago was part of the Spiritual World. You went into the Invisible World and brought something into this Visible World. This process also applies to what you think and what you say. The origin of these three actions is in the Spiritual Universe.

It might take a couple of reads to understand this, but the explanation above is very powerful. If you are able to understand that what you **think, say, and write** all start in the Spiritual World, you can use them as tools to go in and out the Spiritual Universe, and start manifesting your desires with these three actions. This is why it is so important to write your goals and desires on a piece of paper. There is so much more going on than just a cute little laundry list of desires. You are truly being a creator of experiences. You can only attract more of what you are already being—a creator.

What you think

Be conscious of your thoughts. Have you noticed that about 70% of the thoughts you have throughout the day are either not necessary or they are hindering your current situation? Any thought you are creating toward scarcity, fear, anxiety, stress, anger, etc. will create more of the same. Any thoughts, such as, "I am late to work... This weather sucks... Work is so busy and demanding... I have no life... I have no time... I don't like this... This is not fair... That person is so stupid... etc.," are just creating and manifesting more of the same into your life.

What you say

Have you truly paid attention to the way you speak? What type of words do you choose to use? Are you using a vocabulary that reflects stress, anger, anxiety, scarcity, or hatred? Or is your vocabulary reflecting words of happiness, love, peace, and joy? What type of phrases or conversations do you tend to have with others and with yourself? Have you noticed that most people's conversations and their most used words are words and phrases like: "**Ugh**, today is Monday... This weather **sucks**... It is too cold... It is too hot... I was **stuck** in traffic... I eat like **shit**... I feel like **shit**... **This always happens to me**... I **never** get to the train on time... I **never** win... I **always** feel this **pain...** I **never** have **time**... I am **always sick**... Things are **too expensive**... I **don't have** enough **money**... I **hate it** when... I **don't like** "X" about this person... I am **such an idiot**... I am **not really good at that**... I **suck** at that... I am **not** creative, I am **(insert any negative word in here: fat, lazy, dumb, slow, etc.)** ... etc."

Most people tend to say things that they don't like. Again, they are using one of the powers of manifestation to create more of the same, which in this case is more of what they don't want. Is this happening to you? Be honest with yourself.

Your subconscious mind is always listening. It doesn't know the difference between a joke, sarcasm, or something you truly mean. By saying all these negative words in your life, you are not only creating more of the same, but you are also programming your subconscious mind; you are making a habit of *being* those negative commands. Use your language carefully.

Focus your energy on using kind and loving words toward yourself and others, and even toward circumstances outside of you. Especially be mindful about anything that comes right after the words "I am…"

Chapter 3

The Power of the Brain

Habits

A habit is a set of automatic, unconscious thoughts, behaviours, and emotions acquired through repetition. These actions were first processed by your conscious mind but are now performed by your subconscious mind. Our brain is full of habits that run 95% of our lives. Everything, from brushing your teeth to walking, talking, driving, using your cell phone, showering, eating, your job, etc., is habits—even feelings are habits. But habits go way deeper than this. Your name, personality, identity, the way you think, your beliefs, being constantly healthy or constantly sick, being angry, feeling stressed, what you think you don't like, etc. are also habits.

Every day when you wake up in the morning, consciously and subconsciously, your brain grabs information from its surroundings to remind you of who you think you are. You repeat information, such as your name, your gender, you age, where you are from, and your personality. Therefore, you have created the habit of thinking that you are this *persona* you have come so familiarized to believe that you are. But remember, a habit is a thought, behaviour, and emotion that you keep repeating over and over again, until it is being run by your subconscious mind. In other words, your subconscious mind doesn't need you anymore. It can run the show by itself, and as a matter of fact, it does. This is how 95% of your life is being run on autopilot. So if, every day, you choose to *repeat ideas and thoughts,* such as your name, your age, your *social status,* what you like and what you do not like, etc., you eventually create a habit of believing that you are these thoughts; and now you are truly convinced that you are who you think are.

Now imagine creating a habit of believing in limiting ideas (this is where things get really interesting). Imagine thinking over and over again about an experience that hurt you in the past, a physical or emotional pain, or a memory of someone telling you that you are not good enough or strong enough. Imagine repeating thoughts that don't serve you in your head. Perhaps you tell yourself and others the story that you didn't get the love you wanted from your parents or from your siblings, or from other people you looked up to; or that perhaps you are not deserving of love or anything good in this world. Imagine repeating thoughts and feelings of lack, sadness, anger, stress, and anxiety. Imagine repeating the feelings of anxiety, frustration, disappointment, and hatred, because those are the feelings you felt in a lot of the circumstances and experiences you had in your life—anything from being stuck in traffic to actually experiencing something really hard to believe. Repetition of these feelings is how you are creating a habit of them.

Are you able to become aware that those limiting ideas and negative emotions you choose to run in your head and pay attention to, become habits that get triggered every day of your life? As I mentioned before, even feelings become habits. Whether you like it or not, whether you are aware of it or not, the repetition of any thought or feeling will become a habit. Your brain will create the neuro-patterns and neuro-connections to make any thought or feeling you keep repeating, a habit; and the habit will get stronger and stronger, the more you reinforce it.

I understand that you didn't know you were consciously doing this. I understand that this was not your intention. You and I we're not taught how to build the right set of habits, and I am not talking about brushing your teeth, showering, eating your vegetables, etc. I'm talking about the habits of happiness, love, peace, joy, abundance, freedom, health, wealth, feeling in-love with life, and feeling powerful, creative, and whole. Yes, health is a habit; wealth is a habit—all of these are habits. Even experiencing miracles in your life is a habit you can now choose to create.

Our brain is programmed to create habits to make our life easier. It is designed to create a comfort zone so that you and I can feel *safe*. If you feel safe, you could then learn new things, grow, and evolve. If you feel *safe*, it means you are not living in *survival mode;* you are living in *creative mode.* (You read about these two states of beings in Chapter 2 – Illusions.) But the reality is that you have pushed too far this habit of wanting to stay in a comfort zone. Without even knowing it, you are using your brain to create the habit of staying comfortable. This is not the purpose of life. You are meant to always be growing. You are meant to always be expanding, to be more and to have more. You are an unlimited being with exponential potential. And just like a tree grows as much as it can, you're supposed to do the same; we are a reflection of nature. And if you stay in this "comfort zone" for too long, life will present you with a challenging experience that you might see as suffering and/or painful, but the experience is just a message of love from the Divine Intelligence, reminding you that you are meant for so much more. You might have already experienced a few of these challenging situations throughout your life. I know I did. These experiences will help you grow and evolve. Remember that physics states that energy is always in constant movement; you can never make it static. You are meant to keep on growing, expanding, and becoming more and more.

Your Subconscious Mind (the Program)

Now you know that 95% of what you are is a habit, and that your brain is designed to create habits. So, walking, driving, taking public transportation, the way you react to things, the way you get angry in traffic, the anxiety you feel when running "late" to work, even your income, your thoughts around money, your need to always be doing something, feeling stressed, your need to control, your need of knowing what *the plan* is all the time, your diet, working out (or not), the way you relate to lovers in a relationship, etc.… everything in your life is a habit. And if you are not in the present, fully aware of all the miracles around you, knowing that every second you experience is a new moment that you have not yet experienced, your brain is running a subconscious program—a "computer" program you have previously designed for your subconscious mind to run. Trust me, you are just being told what to do; you are in the passenger's seat most of the time.

So, how can you reprogram your mind? How can you start creating the good kind of habits—the habits that will make you happier, healthier, richer, more at peace, in-love with life, etc.— the habits you were never taught how to program? Or maybe you have the right programs, and this will be a reinforcement to your already good habits.

Based on the incredible work of Dr. Bruce Lipton, you are able to reprogram your mind in two different ways. Here is my understanding and experience on the subject.

Your Conscious Mind

Your conscious mind is your brain in action; it is active when you are in the present moment, when you are aware of your thoughts and feelings, and when you are aware of what is happening every second of your life. Your conscious mind learns by repetition, like when you were learning how to ride a bike, or how to drive a car, etc. It is slow, but through repetition, it builds neuro-patterns that eventually get pushed into your subconscious mind, where information gets stored and used as part of your nature. This happens over a long period of time, but this is one way you can reprogram your subconscious mind.

Making anything a habit is a matter of time, and whether you are aware of it or not, and whether you like it or not, you are always practising something. Remember this: Time will make you an expert at *something*. Your responsibility is to choose what that *something* is. If you live as a victim, you will become an expert at living as a victim. Things will happen to you, and most likely you will be tuning into feelings of anger, sadness, stress, anxiety, and hatred. On the contrary, if you choose to live as a creator, you will become an expert at being the owner of your life, and you will create miracles. Things will happen for you, and you will most likely be tuning into feelings of happiness, love, abundance, peace, and joy.

Start by creating the repetitive action of being grateful. This is the easiest way to start changing your habits. We all have so much to be grateful for, especially the things that most people take for granted. Can you breathe? Can you taste food? Can you listen to music? Is your heart beating? Are your lungs taking the right amount of air for you to survive? Are you able to experience a new day in which everything is possible? Are you able to perhaps say "I love you" to a family member, your partner, or a pet? Do you have a job? Do you not have a job (this is perfect too!)? I could fill up hundreds of pages giving you examples of what to be grateful for.

At the end of the day, what matters the most is learning how to activate the feeling of gratitude. It is learning to be humble. It is learning how to focus your attention on gratitude, and if you are able to focus on this and truly feel gratitude, guess what's going to come into your life—more things and more experiences that will make you feel grateful. When you truly see everything around you as a miracle, you understand and feel that you are experiencing "heaven on earth." All you have is this moment, and you can do with it anything you want.

Every morning before you get out of bed, and every night before you fall asleep, make a mental list of everything you are grateful for; think about it and feel it. Yes, you have heard this before, but I hope that with everything you have read up until now, and will continue to read, you will understand that you are activating the Divine Energy within you, you are creating and reinforcing new neuro-patterns in your brain. You are teaching your body and your cells to feel gratitude, and a lot more than just a cute little thank-you-list is happening around and inside of you when you do this simple exercise. Most importantly, create the habit of knowing what gratitude *feels* like.

You can do this same exercise with the feelings of love, happiness, abundance, and peace. You can think about the things you love, the things that bring you peace, and the experiences that make you happy. You can feel all the abundance that is already inside and outside of you. These exercises are meant to help your brain create new neuro-patterns that will then become habits. And by the way, you are not only teaching your brain how to make a habit of these feelings, you are also imprinting your cells with the energy that these emotions carry. That's right; you are creating chemical reactions in your body (through your feelings) that start changing your DNA.

Your Subconscious Mind

Your subconscious mind is like a computer program where there is no one behind the wheel. It is an autopilot program that is operating your body and brain whenever you are not paying attention to the present moment (which might be 95% of the time).

Babies from the age of 0–2 learn through hypnosis. Their subconscious mind is a giant sponge that learns through hypnosis. Picture a one-year-old baby boy: He gets taken everywhere; he goes with the flow; he is not able to do anything by himself. All he does is look out into the world, in a hypnotic state; and he learns from the energy of his surroundings. His subconscious mind takes it all in and creates neuro-patterns and habits out of the energy he perceives and receives from the outer world. This is why it is very important that parents become aware of how they feel, and the energy they put out around their babies. These little ones will learn by energy alone; whether a parent is trying to hide a negative emotion or not, the baby will sense it, learn from it, and will imprint any emotion in his cells.

Even though you will never be 0–2 years old again, you can program your subconscious mind through hypnosis again. There are two times during the day where your brain falls into the same hypnotic state that a baby lives in. The first one is the moment you are waking up in the morning, those 5–10 minutes that you're still in a dream state, but you are also almost awake. You are neither here nor there. You are half asleep and half awake. The other moment is the last 5–10 minutes of your day. As you are going into your sleep, there are about three to five minutes where your *conscious mind* lets go, but your *unconscious mind* has not completely kicked in or taken over. Again, you are neither here nor there.

These two moments are by far the most important times of the day. I would even say that the last five minutes before you go to bed are the most important time of your day. If your life is run 95% by subconscious thoughts that you have planted in your brain, it might be a good idea to start reprogramming your brain to have subconscious thoughts related to abundance, health, wealth, happiness, peace, love, etc.

Let's take a look at what happens in those last five minutes of the day before you go to bed…

Most of the time, you might go to bed thinking one of two things:

One, you are either thinking about a future based on a past (you will learn about your past future in the following pages): all the things you need to do tomorrow, all the people you have to see, the things you have to do, that deadline that is coming up, the clients you need to see, the bills you need to pay, the projects you need to deliver, the news you are going to hear about tomorrow, etc. You are worried about all this information that was created in the past, of which you are expecting to live it tomorrow (a future based on your past).

Or two, you might be stuck on a memory of the past, which is causing you anger or sadness. You are thinking about something or someone that made you angry, frustrated, or sad. You are thinking of an experience where you didn't quite like the outcome. You might be sad or angry about something someone either said or did "to you," and you are caught in an eternal loop of feeling and thinking these negative thoughts. You are simply thinking of a bad experience before you go to bed.

No matter which one of the above thoughts are running through your head, you are filling up your head with stress, anger, sadness, and anxiety, right before you fall asleep. Well, guess what? As you fall asleep, during those last five minutes before you doze off into your dreams, you are programming your subconscious mind with feelings and thoughts of stress, anxiety, anger, lack, and sadness. You are chemically imprinting emotions into your body and subconscious mind to remember and create habits related to those emotions. You are creating a program based on stress, fear, anger, and anxiety. So, if most of your day is run by your subconscious mind (your program), your body and brain will seek experiences that will bring you more of the same. You will subconsciously seek experiences that would make you feel those same negative feelings you are subconsciously craving. This is why it is so hard to start a new diet or to start going to the gym; or perhaps you keep dating the same kind of negative people, even though you don't want to. Subconsciously, you have programmed yourself to seek these negative experiences—your body craves them.

This is why it is so hard to "change" from a conscious level. Again, how many times have you tried to lose those extra pounds and perhaps couldn't? How many times have you tried changing your diet, or waking up earlier, or really going to the gym as part of your routine? How many times have you tried giving up an unhealthy habit, or being more positive, etc.? Consciously, you might be ready, and you could possess all the knowledge you need in order to make all those changes in your life: you read the books, watched the videos, signed up for that gym membership, etc. You had the right intention, yet you were not able to get to your goal. Your subconscious mind has created the habits of what you do not want in your life, and this program is very strong. Remember, 95% of human life is run by a subconscious program. If you want to change your life, you need to change the program.

This is why the last five minutes of the day, before you fall asleep, must be filled with thoughts that clearly intend for your biggest wishes to be fulfilled, along with the feelings and the elevated emotions that accompany such thoughts. The combination of the thought with the corresponding feeling is very important. So, instead of running a list of things through your head that you *think* you need to do tomorrow, imagine the experiences and dreams you really desire to live. This time is sacred; it is for you and you only. Do not let anyone or anything into this time, unless you want to experience more of the same. As you doze off into the unconscious dreamland, clearly imagine what it would feel like to have or be what you truly desire to experience in this life. You might want to say and feel things like (again, feeling is key in this process) "I am happy," "I am wealthy," "I am healthy," "I am love," "I am prosperous," "I am inner peace," "I am... ZzZzZz...

The more you do this, the easier it will get. It definitely takes time to become aware of everything that's happening inside of you. But the key here is to create a habit of remembering all these little details so that you will never let any negative thought or feeling you don't want to experience, run through both your conscious and your subconscious mind.

Living in the Past

I always thought I was living in the present moment—I wasn't. I always thought that when people referred to *"living in the present moment,"* I knew what they meant—I didn't. It wasn't until I heard Dr. Joe Dispenza talk about the following concepts in his book, *Becoming Supernatural*, that I understood what the present moment really means. It wasn't until I started to understand that who I think I am is all based on memories, information, and habitual behaviours of the past: my identity, my name, my age, my gender, my race, my nationality, etc., that I started to realize how to call my attention back into this present moment. Think about this for a second: If everything you do in this present moment is based on the information created in the past, you are not living in the present moment. Therefore, you can say that you are currently living a present-based-on-your-past. Let me try to further explain this.

As soon as you wake up in the morning, your brain starts gathering information from its environment; this happens consciously and subconsciously, and it happens very fast. It rapidly starts to fire up old neuro-connections (neuro-patterns that have grown stronger over the years as you keep activating them over and over again) so that you can identify with your name, gender, age, current location, your spouse or partner, what day it is, what you do for a living, the things you need to do for the day, etc. This happens so fast that you're not aware of it. This happens even before you have time to get out of bed and walk to the washroom (we saw this example in the previous chapter).

All this information is based on experiences and events from your past. All this information was created and experienced, not today but days, weeks, months, and perhaps years ago. You have started your day based on the past. Your entire identity was created and exists in your past. I cannot put enough emphasis on this: The minute your brain recognizes your name, gender, age, location, relationships, etc., you are living your life in the *past-present*.

By simply remembering all this information, which you have accumulated over the years, your starting point is where you left it—yesterday, your past. This is why it is so hard, and almost impossible, to create a new future. Because every day, without you even knowing it, you start your day in the past. And because you keep doing this, your future is always going to look very similar to your past. You might as well take what happened last Tuesday, press "copy" and "paste," and place the *old* Tuesday on the Tuesdays to follow—unless you learn how to live life from your natural state of being: a present moment creator.

There is one more element to add to how you live in the past. Every person, thing, circumstance, and event in your life (like work, your group of friends, your coworkers, your boss, your daily commute, your family, etc.) has an emotion or feeling attached to it. Every time you either meet someone for the first time or you have a new experience, your brain, consciously and subconsciously, categorizes this new information for you. Your brain then creates a judgement of this new event based on your past—you subconsciously compare this new event to other similar events you have previously experienced. This helps you make sense of this new event. Your brain then creates feelings and emotions that get chemically stored in your body and in your brain.

The emotions and feelings that you have created and stored toward a certain person or experience in your life, are brought back into your life experience every single time you either **see** or **even think** about this person or event. This is how powerful your brain is; even if you are just thinking about a certain person or experience, your brain activates the neuro-patterns related to this event, and it starts to chemically reproduce the feelings and emotions you felt when you were experiencing this past event. You can actually feel as if you are re-living this experience, or as if you are in front of this person, even though this is just happening by thought alone. This is why most cannot get past beyond something that happened in their lives; they cannot move on from an experience, such as a break-up, being fired, losing a bunch of money, a friend's "betrayal," etc. They keep re-living the experience over and over again by just thinking about it. They are recreating the same past feelings and emotions they experienced when the event happened for the first time. The body thinks this event is happening right now. And yes, this is definitely happening to you as well. Dr. Joe Dispenza, author of the book, *Becoming Supernatural*, says:

"The body cannot distinguish between an experience that happens in real life and an experience that is created by thought alone."

Here is a quick example of how this works:

Think of a co-worker you really like. I'm sure you can recall nice feelings and thoughts attached to this person. If you close your eyes and picture this individual, I'm sure the feelings attached to this person will get stronger and more vivid the more you think about him or her. These feelings and emotions were created by you, and stored chemically in your body. And because they exist in a memory in your body, you are able to feel them again just by thought alone, even though this person is not in front of you right now. This person only exists in your thoughts right now, yet you are feeling the emotions attached to this person as if he or she were in front of you. On the contrary, I'm sure you can also think of someone at work that might cause the opposite feelings from the ones you have with the one co-worker you like (someone you might now like). Can you think of one person you don't necessarily like or relate to at work? Oops, you are now feeling the not-so-good kind of feelings—sorry.

So, this is how you are living your life in the past: thinking that you are living in the present moment but are truly living in the *past-present*. By simply acknowledging your name, gender, age, relationships, work, etc., you are living today based on your yesterday. I understand that you might feel confused. Just wait until I explain what living in the *future-based-on-your-past* means. But don't worry; I promise that it will all make sense, and you will understand how to unplug your attention from the past and/or future, and see the world as one eternal moment full of wonder and miracles. You will know how to be aware that every single moment in your life is a new moment. You will create the consciousness and awareness that there is no such thing as an ordinary moment.

Living in the Future-Based-on-Your-Past

Living in the *present-based-on-your-past,* and living in the *future-based-on-your-past,* are hopefully eye-openers that are meant to elevate your awareness of what is happening in your life, so that you can create a mind that lives in the true *present.* Being aware of what you are feeling and what you are thinking about all the time, is how you will create the awareness and the consciousness of living in this moment, so that you can tap into your Divine Energy to create the future you really want.

Living in the future-based-on-your-past

If at any point you think about tomorrow, or your future, and you feel fear, anxiety, anger, or stress, it means that you are thinking of a future based on a past. For example, if you think about Mondays, and you get irritated and angry because "you have to go to work," you only feel angry because you are recalling that perhaps work is not a place where you want to be on Mondays. You have created a negative connotation toward work and toward Mondays. And these memories and/or feelings were created in the past; therefore, you are basing what you are going to experience tomorrow on feelings and emotions created in the past. I think you start to get the picture. If you look at tomorrow and feel any negative emotion, it's only because you are choosing to see your *tomorrow* (future) in a similar way as your *yesterday* (past).

This applies to any experience: Will I get this job if I apply for it? Will I get the money I need to pay for what I need? Is this going to be OK? If you do not feel excitement for a tomorrow that you have not yet experienced, it is because you have already decided that your future is going to look like your past.

Please understand that what lies in your future is prosperity, happiness, love, peace, and joy. Life has nothing other than abundance and love waiting for you. But if you decide not to move past the information you have collected in your brain, you won't be able to experience the miracles that you are meant to live. Let go of any past information you have recorded in your brain. It is all an illusion. Tomorrow is full of infinite possibilities. Trust.

Breaking the Habit of Being Yourself

I hope that throughout this book, you are finding some of the answers you have been looking for, or that you are at least acquiring a new perspective. Over the next few chapters, we will start to go deeper into the concepts that talk about how you relate to all the energy of the Universe, and the concepts of miracles and magic. For now, I want to talk about a very important detail: In order to live your heart's desires, you're going to have to break the habit of being yourself.

Being yourself has gotten you to where you are right now. This is a good place. No matter what the circumstances around you are—perhaps there's physical or emotional pain; perhaps there's stress or anxiety in your life; or perhaps you're not where you want to be (or maybe you are)— there is still a lot to be grateful for. You are here in this moment in time and space because of who you have chosen to believe you are. And in order to experience what you truly want—that freedom, that health, that prosperity or that level of abundance—you must realize and be honest with yourself that this person you are desiring to be is not the personality you have built so far.

Most people want to get to their desires and wishes from the same place they are standing right now. What they don't realize is that this is not possible. You cannot be at Point B when you are currently standing at Point A. In order to be at Point B (living your perfect life), you have to be the person that lives in that Point B reality. You cannot be the same person you are right now. You cannot be the same person that lives in Point A reality but experiences the life that Point B reality has to offer. You simply have to let go of who you are right now; the YOU at Point A is not the same YOU that exists at Point B. You have to let go of everything you know.

Breaking this habit of being yourself is letting go of who you think you are. It is understanding that you are not defined by who you have thought to be up to this point. Everything you have accumulated this far is not you. All the thoughts you have thought, and all the emotions you have felt, have gotten you to right *here* and right *now*. And if right *here,* and right *now,* are not exactly what you would like to be experiencing, you have to let go of the ideas, thoughts, and emotions that have gotten you to this point in time and space. You have to redefine who you are.

As I mentioned earlier in this chapter, you must be open to the fact that you have most likely created the habit of being angry, doubtful, stressed, anxious, and fearful most of the time. You must be open to the possibility that if your reality is not exactly what you want it to be, you have subconscious programs and repetitive patterns that keep you attached to this reality. You have not yet created the right kind of programs and habits that can get you to where you truly belong—you have not yet created the habits of happiness, abundance, love, joy, peace, health, and wealth.

Be patient with yourself. This part of the book is simply meant to try to open your mind to the reality that there are subconscious programs and habits running your life, and that there is a way to program your brain and create the right habits. This part of the book is meant to open your heart to take a deep dive inside of you and, once and for all, join the happiness, love, peace and abundance that has always been there, waiting for you to join the club. This Source Energy does not judge. This Love Force doesn't have favourites—it can't. It is always there for everyone and anyone that allows it into their lives.

Please understand that you are still going to feel every range of emotions. You are still going to "get hit" by life (I promise it is not an actual "hit" but a message of love). You are still living in this physical world, with a physical body, which will experience all kinds of feelings, some good and some bad—I still experience all kinds of feelings. But now you can always decide how long you are going to stay with those negative feelings inside of you. As a mentor once told me:

"It is OK to fall into the pool.
People drown because they decide to stay in the pool."
– James MacNeil

How long are you going to feel that negative emotion? I can assure you that in the past, a negative emotion or experience stuck with me for a very long time: days, weeks, months, even years. Now I'm training my body and my mind to move on from a bad experience, within minutes. Nothing is forever. And the sooner you understand that you are going to trip a few times along the way, the better. What matters is how long it takes you to get up again and keep moving, and trust that you are on the right path.

Make a conscious commitment to break the habit of being yourself. Remember, you are not who you think you are. You are not your name, gender, age, ethnicity—you are not even your body—you are not the identity you so strongly fight to keep and protect. You simply are, you simply exist, you simply experience... Let me say this one more time... You simply are.

If you bring your attention and your energy to this present moment, you can begin to feel how there is only one eternal moment. It is only once you exist inside this eternal moment that you are able to leave behind everything you have been holding on to in the past. It is only in this eternal moment that you can clearly see that you are always a blank canvas. Again, you just simply are...

I know you have a dream life, a life in which abundance is present in every single aspect of your life: love, finance, health, career, family, material stuff, happiness, spirituality, etc. This dream life of yours does exist. You and I are all capable of living this life; it is in our Divine Nature to live a Divine Life. If you are not experiencing abundance in all aspects of your life, this means you have to break the habit of being yourself. The *YOU* that is living that dream life, is not the *you* that is perhaps reading this book right now. You have to let go of the *YOU* that you are right now, in order to find the *YOU* that is living that dream life. Your life right now was created by *your persona,* and your dream life is being experienced by *a different persona*—a new *YOU.* A new life can never be created from the old life. The new you cannot be created from the old you. You have to let go of who you think you are.

I understand this is hard to grasp and put into practice. These last words are only meant to highlight that everything you can ever imagine is possible. You have to be open to reconstructing who you think you are. I know I already started this process. I go in and out between my *NEW* and my *OLD* self. My point is, perhaps one day I can only live from my *NEW* me; maybe one day I will stop jumping in and out. One day I will simply be this *new* me.

Chapter 4

Childlike Wonder

"All children are artists.
The problem is how to remain an artist once they grow up."
– Pablo Picasso

Kids Know the Truth

Remember when you were a kid? Remember flying to space on top of a unicorn?

I am going to let you in on a little secret. Between the ages of two and seven, you and I understood that there was a Divine Source of energy living inside of us—an unlimited, powerful, infinite energy, with no beginning and no end. This energy inside of you knows that you came into this world to create and experience anything you can possibly imagine. This energy knows how to attract miracles into your life. As kids, you and I understood that the way to communicate with this energy was through imagination, playfulness, happiness, and joy. These emotions are essential to the manifestation process. Imagination and feelings are the language of the Universe and manifestation, not words and reactions.

You and I used to always use this innate understanding. But as you and I grew up, we were pushed into a box. You were told to grow up and to stop playing games. Perhaps it was your parents, or your older siblings. Perhaps it was society and the fear you experienced once you started to put yourself out there. No one is to blame here. Trust me, they didn't do it on purpose; it was not their intention to create separation between you and this Source Energy of love, peace, and joy. They also didn't know this was happening. Just like you, they were just following a social limited pattern that was forced into their subconscious program.

Don't worry; the good news is that this Divine Energy never left. It is part of you, and it is always there. And you already know this, because you can feel it. You feel it every time you laugh at a joke, or when you dance, or whenever you are with family or friends having a great time. You can feel this energy every time you are at a concert, watching an inspiring movie, listening to your favourite songs, painting, drawing, exercising, baking, cooking, etc.—you name it, whenever you are having fun, you can feel this Divine Energy inside of you again. Whenever you stop thinking about time and space, and the only thing that matters is what you are doing in the moment, you are back to talking to that inner Force. But perhaps you forgot how to play, how to imagine, how to have fun, how not to worry about the illusion of problems—don't worry, we will talk about that too.

A big key of manifestation and creating magic in your life is to learn how to live in this state of wonder again. You have to re-learn how to be in this state all day long—and yes, this is possible. This is your natural state of being: playfulness, happiness, love, peace, and joy. You were never taught how to tap into this energy on a constant basis. You were never taught how to focus your thoughts and emotions to be in this state of being all the time. You were never taught how to create the habit of happiness, love, peace, and joy. I will talk about how to permanently be in this state of being, in Chapter 10 – Real Magic.

Childlike Wonder

I've always been fascinated by watching kids and babies interact with the world around them. It's such a beautiful thing to sit back and observe how babies and kids start to become aware of their surroundings. Next time you are around a kid or a baby, just sit back and ask yourself, "What is he or she thinking right now?" They are so fascinated by everything around them. They want to touch, play, explore, and try everything! And they never get tired! This is called *childlike wonder*. Do you remember what that feels like?

When kids see a magic trick for the first few times, something incredible happens in their heads. These little guys are just getting used to some of the "rules" of our reality, such as how *objects are not meant to just disappear or appear out of thin air.* Then, as they watch the trick happen, they have a quick little moment where something completely different happens in front of their eyes—an experience they don't quite understand.

Most kids believe this experience is magical, and they just accept it. There is a part of them that truly believes that *"the coin manifested from behind their ear,"* or that *"something disappeared or appeared out of thin air."* Kids are not trying to figure out the method, nor are they questioning what is happening. They are simply in the moment, astonished by what they just saw.

Have you noticed how people tend to be happier around babies? Notice how you and the rest of the family seem to gravitate toward a baby or a kid. You might call his or her name, showing the baby a new toy, or perhaps you might be making a funny face or acting silly (sorry) just to grab the kid's attention. This happens because something inside of you gets triggered on a subconscious level. You remember what it was like to be a kid, where seeing anything new awakened a sense of curiosity, fun, and wonder. Everything around you seemed new and interesting. For example, when you see a kid experience something for the first time (like learning how to ride a bicycle for example), it reminds you, again on a subconscious level, how much fun it was to live life free, not worrying about anything, and enjoying everything—no bills to pay, no responsibilities (I guess you did have one responsibility after all: fun).

Discovering the world is an amazing adventure that you may have forgotten how to experience. You may have forgotten to truly live and see the world with childlike wonder. At least I did for a while. I was unaware that this had happened. I was so unaware of it that I had convinced myself that I was happy. But deep inside, there was a little voice, a very quiet one, asking:

"Why am I not as happy as I say I am? Where did my childlike wonder go? Where did that joy, passion, and whimsical creativity go that I had when I was a kid? Where did the magic go?"

When I am on stage giving my lecture on my take on magic, or when I perform magic for people, I can see and feel people's childlike wonder. I can see the spark that reminds them that anything is possible, the energy that reminds them to live in that state of discovery and creation. You and I are meant to live in fun, joy, happiness, and playfulness. You deserve to create and experience anything you want. And the kid inside of you knows this. So... remind yourself to be a kid again. Remind yourself of the experience of flying to space on top of a unicorn. You are worthy of it.

The Child Inside of You

It's very interesting to observe that the older we get, we somehow stop being amazed by everything that happens around us. We *get used to* this illusion of life. The feeling of wonder and astonishment diminishes, and sometimes it disappears. When and why did you and I *"get used to"* taking life for granted? Why do you think this happens? Why do you and I find it so hard to feel wonder and astonishment every single day?

Imagine a kid, perhaps a little boy. Imagine him waking up in the morning. Let's pretend that today is excursion day at school; he is going to the zoo. This little boy probably woke up very early (even before his parents), full of energy and excitement, ready to live the day. He is very excited about the fact that he is going to see all kinds of different animals at the zoo. He's probably thinking about giraffes, zebras, elephants, and lions. He didn't even sleep that much the night before. He has already imagined many adventures in his head. He probably got all dressed up even before his parents told him to do so, and he is ready to go. This is childlike wonder in its purest form. This is being in love with life, in love with the moment and the discovery of new things—knowing that there is something unknown and new around every corner. This boy is excited to live his day because there is nothing *expected* about it. In his head, he can only imagine the exciting adventures ahead of him. He is only experiencing feelings of joy, excitement, and wonder. He can't wait to experience *today*.

This is how you and I should feel every day. Take your routine, for example, like going to work. This action of waking up and getting ready to go to work should feel like *"going to the zoo,"* like it did for this little boy. The reason you wake up in the morning and probably don't jump out of bed and rush out the door to live your day, is because you are most likely able to predict every single event that is about to happen in your day. You've already imagined how today is going to play out, and you have left all the excitement and sense of wonder out of it. You have based your *today* on your *past*. And if you take your habits of the past, and you repeat them today, there is nothing new and exciting to live.

I do want you to be aware that this decision of looking at the day without excitement and a sense of wonder is only happening in your head. You are making the decision to make no room for the unexpected. Therefore, there is no room for any adventure to happen in your life. You have created a habit of paying attention to your routine. That's all it is—a habit of thinking about what appears to be a routine in your life. All you see is what you pay attention to. You have to stop putting your attention on what feels like a routine. Because *the feeling* of routine is just an illusion— the day you are about to live has not happened yet.

A routine is only a thought you have chosen to create in your mind. Every moment of every day is new. There is nothing repetitive when you live your life in the now. You have to be aware of this. You have to create the consciousness that life is just one eternal moment that you are experiencing. Recognize that *right now* only exists in the unknown. It is your senses and your brain that try to categorize *today* as a routine. Your five senses are trying to make you feel "safe" so that you can feel comfortable with everything around you, and so that you can feel a sense of control. But by thinking and feeling that everything is a routine, you create the habit of boredom and lack of astonishment.

You have also been pushed to think that something new is scary, another habit you have to get rid of. Your natural state of being, is discovery and adventure, like the little boy going to the zoo, in the example above. Everything you experienced as a child was new, exciting, and wonderful; yet today, you are choosing to experience the same thoughts, which lead to the same feelings, which lead to the same actions, which lead to the same outcome. There is only one constant in this life, and that is change. Change is always happening, whether you like it or not, and whether you are aware of it or not. Nothing can, and will not, stay the same. Put your awareness into the infinite possibilities that exist in the unknown. Get excited about what could happen, and stop living in fear. Fear is just another illusion.

Practice childlike wonder with everything around you. There is no such thing as a routine. Bring your attention to the joy, curiosity, playfulness, and fun of everything that is new (which is everything in front of you). This is a powerful exercise to practice all the time. This is how you start gaining back your childlike wonder power. Be curious about everything; be playful with everything. Sing, laugh, dance, paint, play, run, yell, discover, learn, explore, and invent. Put your awareness into what you are doing by being grateful that you are back to being in touch with this inner part of you that knows how to be playful and adventurous; it will only get more powerful. You will start to feel so much joy for life. You will start to feel an incontrollable need to play again, and to rediscover what it is like to live in this natural state of discovery, fun, and adventure. Go play!

Never. Stop. Playing.

The way a kid learns to communicate with his/her inner world is through playing. This is a personal space of discovery and connection to Source that cannot be reached by anyone else but the kid himself/herself. Let's take a little girl, for example. When a little girl plays with her toys, she is living inside her imagination. She places mental pictures and creates feelings of infinite possibilities. She is using pure energy to connect to her inner-self, to create a perfect world, a world where everything is possible—**a happy place**.

You and I have been raised to believe that kids are the only ones that are allowed to play. As you grow up, your brain has been implanted with phrases such as: "We are not playing right now," "Stop playing," "You have to stop being a kid at some point," "Grow up," "Playing doesn't pay the bills," "You have to get a real job," "This is not the time to play," etc. Through all this repetition of statements, and the energy that is placed around these limiting beliefs, you and I have forgotten that playing is essential to discovering what we like and what we don't like. Playing is essential to connecting with that Divine Energy inside of us, which knows that everything is possible. Playing gives you the room to discover who you truly are; and it is not only an activity meant for kids. Playing is key for you to attract and manifest magic in your own life, regardless of your age.

I am now practicing what it is like to play again. If, as a kid, you used to like to draw, paint, sing, sew, dance like no one was watching, talk to animals or plants, jump around, etc., start playing again. I can promise you that you will start to re-discover what you like about life. Even your goals will start to shift. What you thought was important might take a different meaning. You will reconnect with your inner child. You will reconnect with that inner part of you that knows how to create everything from nothing. Just pick up that pencil, those old dancing shoes, that old yarn, and play. You will find yourself more inspired, more in-sync. That kid that knows the truth about living a life of happiness, love, peace, and joy, is still inside, waiting for you to bring down all the limiting beliefs you decided to accept as truths (which are only someone else's limiting ideas of what they thought life is supposed to be). Please remember, we live in a world ruled by limiting beliefs created by a limited physical mind. You are unlimited by nature; you are Divine Energy.

All I want to do in this chapter is open the possibility for you to be aware of the following: It's not that kids don't know any better; it's not that kids have nothing to worry about and adults do. It's not that kids have less responsibilities than adults; perhaps kids do know the truth. Perhaps kids know that life is meant to be a playground of infinite possibilities, and all of these ideas about jobs, bills to pay, and chores to do are just big illusions that others created for us, and you and I just decided to live them as truths.

Never. Stop. Playing.

Chapter 5

Principles of Magic

Misdirection

Before we go into the topic of misdirection, I would like you to understand the following concept. It is a concept I have previously mentioned in this book, but it is very important to understand:

> *"Where you place your attention,*
> *is where you place your energy."*
> **– Dr. Joe Dispenza**

For example, if you place your attention on what happened yesterday at work, perhaps something that made you feel very stressed or anxious, you are giving away your energy to your past, and you are placing your energy on thoughts and feelings that are not beneficial to the present you. You are giving your energy away to a time that doesn't exist anymore, and you are wasting your energy. So remember, where you place your attention, is where you place your energy. This is a key concept to manifestation and creating miracles in your life.

Misdirection is such an interesting topic in magic. It is key to giving the spectator the experience of magic.

Misdirection is to draw someone's attention to one thing, to distract it from another. Something important to mention here is that if you are watching a magic trick, and you start noticing that something sneaky is going on, I have failed at creating misdirection. If you become aware of a magician doing something "out of the ordinary," he/she has failed at creating true misdirection. When true misdirection happens, you won't even notice it.

There is a big principle of psychology behind misdirection. This principle is that your mind, which is your brain in action, cannot pay attention to two different things at the same time. Think about this for a second. You might think you are able to multitask, but you are not truly able to master any one of the two or more tasks that you are doing simultaneously. Your brain cannot give 100% of its attention to two (or more than two) things at the same time. You are really just dividing your energy into a bunch of things.

This principle of psychology (and of misdirection) is happening right now with everything that you perceive as negative in your life. You have created such a powerful mind (brain in action) that it is only focusing on the things in your life that don't seem to be working for you. Therefore, you are not able to pay attention to what's working in your life. Your brain cannot pay attention to two things at the same time; if you are focusing on the negative, you are not able to pay attention to the positive, the bigger picture. You are not able to understand that happiness, love, peace, and joy are just on the other side of your anger, hatred, and fear.

When you are in a moment of anger, stress, or anxiety, it is very hard to shift your attention to the opposite of what you've trained your brain to focus on. You've created the habit of focusing on the negative. But this can change. If you are able to re-train your mind to be able to focus your attention and keep it on positive feelings, thoughts, and actions, the experience of magic will catch up to you. You will start to see changes and miracles happening in your life. Trust me; this happened to me. Once you re-train your brain to focus on what's working out in your life, everything else starts to follow; everything around you starts to change.

If you could keep your attention only on what's working out for you in your life, for as long as you can, you have no idea how much your life will start to change and transform itself to reflect more wonderful experiences. This is the game: How long can you keep your attention on things that are truly working out for you, leaving out of sight anything that is not?

Puppy vs. Lion

So, we have established that perhaps your attention has been placed in the wrong places. You have been focusing on circumstances, people, and situations that might not necessarily be positive, happy, or peaceful. You have perhaps been giving your attention and your energy to the wrong thoughts and feelings. It's OK, you can start changing this by simply understanding the following. This helped me a lot...

I want you to imagine a cute and playful puppy dog. Imagine him running up and down your house, licking and chewing everything, peeing everywhere and always looking for what else he can play with. Every 20 seconds, this puppy is running around looking for something else to do. **Your attention is like this puppy dog.**

Right now, you are so used to paying attention to so many thoughts (some positive, but mostly negative) that it feels impossible to sit down and just focus on one. You might think that there is so much to think about: work, family, friends, relationships, food, fitness, bills to pay, shows to watch, social media to catch up on, Instagram posts to read and create, news, personal projects, and so on. It seems like there are so many things dividing your attention (your energy), and it seems like it has become quite impossible to focus your energy on one thing. But again, this is all in your head. These are the habits that you have created. It is very important to understand that the key to creating miracles in your life, is learning how to focus *all* your energy (your attention) on one thing at a time, and to do it with purpose.

Here is how to know if your attention is like a puppy dog (which most likely it is). Close your eyes for five minutes; that is right, five minutes (you can do this exercise before going to bed tonight or in the shower if you want—this is just an exercise to find out if your mind is a puppy dog or not). Think *only* about feelings of happiness, love, and peace. Start to feel those emotions inside your body, and just repeat these words over and over again: "I feel love; I feel peaceful; I feel happy." Are you able to do this? Are you able to feel and sustain these feelings for at least five minutes? Do you notice other thoughts popping inside your head, out of nowhere? Are you thinking about that text message you haven't answered, or the social media feed you cannot wait to scroll through? Are you thinking about what you need to do after you finish doing this exercise? Are you thinking about what you need to do tomorrow? Are you thinking about something that's bothering you from two days ago? Perhaps you are thinking of what you need to do for work, which is already past its deadline... You get the idea. If you close your eyes for five minutes, and other thoughts, rather than the feelings of love, peace, and happiness come into your mind, then bingo! Your attention is *a little puppy.*

Now, let's change the image; picture a lioness. Imagine that this magnificent creature is hunting in the wild. She is patiently waiting, focusing all of her energy on her prey, waiting for the right opportunity to attack. This is how your attention should be 24/7. And if at any point during the day, you are feeling either sad, angry, anxious, stressed, etc., it's because you are paying attention to the wrong thing (puppy dog). You have not yet trained yourself to: 1) notice that you are paying attention to the wrong things, 2) shift your attention to a positive thought, and 3) maintain your attention on thoughts and feelings that keep you in what I call our natural state of being, of love, happiness, peace, and joy.

After I understood the difference between what it is like to have an attention span that behaves like a puppy dog and one that behaves like a lioness, I started to wonder that if I could focus my attention (my energy) on the right thoughts and feelings, and that if I could keep this awareness and level of consciousness without any distractions (no doubt, no fear, no anxiety, no stress, no anger), maybe I could change the way I react toward all the events and circumstances in my life, especially the ones that didn't seem to be "working out" for me. It took me a while to be able to do this, but after some work, everything started to shift. I became happier, more peaceful, healthier, filled with energy, and in love with life. No matter what the circumstances outside of me were, good or bad, tense or relaxed, I was able to stay in that natural state of being, of love, happiness, peace, and joy. And yes, this is something you can do too. And yes, this is something that I am still working on and want to master. I have learned that the way you react to what happens on the outside, is purely based on what you have on the inside.

So, how do you go from having a cute little puppy dog attention span, to a fierce and focused lioness attention span? I talk about how to do this, in Chapter 9 – The Habit of Magic. I will show you the steps I took to create a consciousness and awareness that helps me stay in higher vibrations of energy. I am now able to focus and keep my attention, *misdirection*, on the only thought that you and I should always be acknowledging and living life from: the truth that you came into this world to only experience happiness, love, peace, and joy.

"You can either be a host to love, or a hostage to your ego."
– Wayne Dyer

You are always choosing one or the other, whether you like it or not. If you are not focused on your dreams, on feeling good right now, and on paying attention to the correct thoughts and feelings, you are paying attention to the negative kinds of thoughts and feelings. If you are not focusing on your dreams, you are letting the outside world influence your inside world. It is always your choice.

Perception

"Reality is merely an illusion, albeit a very persistent one."
– Albert Einstein

There is no reality; there is just perception. There is no reality; there are only judgements about what is happening.

Perception is a key principle of magic that illustrates how powerful our minds can be. The following is a fact: Magic doesn't happen in my hands; magic happens in your head. I know what the secret is, and how it's done; magic happens in your head.

As a magician, I know that as long as I can create the right environment, your perception of what's happening will do the rest; it will *fill in the blanks* with an inexplicable feeling of magic. It will create the illusion that the impossible just happened.

It is due to your perception of what's happening that the illusion of magic is created. Think about this for a second: There are two perspectives happening in a magic trick. There is the one from the performer, the magician, the one who knows the "secret" to the trick; and there is the one from the observer, you, the spectator who is just creating a subjective experience of what is really happening. There are two realities being created: the one of the magician, who is simply performing a memorized set of actions, and the one you are experiencing, a subjective interpretation of what is simply happening. This does not only apply to a magic trick; this also applies to every single experience happening in your life.

Now let's bring this topic of perception out of magic and into your life experience. As I mentioned in the opening statement of this topic, I invite you to think about the idea that reality doesn't exist, and that what you call reality is just a subjective interpretation of what is happening. Let me elaborate on this. Reality doesn't exist; things are simply experiences that are happening. Think of a house, for example. A house is just the experience of a house. There is no such thing as "my" house or "your" house, or "someone else's" house. Even though we have created the illusion that we buy a piece of land through lawyers, money, etc., a house is simply happening; a house is just the experience of a house—four walls and a roof, which then help us experience what you and I call a house.

Here is a more personal example. There is no such thing as "*your* happiness" or "*my* happiness"; there is just happiness. There is no such thing as "*your* abundance" vs. "*my* abundance"; there is just abundance happening. The more you are able to grasp the concept that you are not you, or that you are not who you think you are, the more you will understand how to connect to all of these wonderful experiences of abundance, happiness, health, wealth, peace, love, etc.

All of these wonderful experiences are simply happening right now, all the time. You cannot attract any of these into your life; you can only experience them by tuning into them. And by understanding that these are *states of being,* and that they can be reached through your perception of things, you can start shaping life to be the experience it is meant to be—a magical and miraculous ride. You are a human ***being;*** you are meant to *be* your desires. You are not a human ***doing;*** you are not meant to struggle and fight to get things. You can start to be all of this right now, with your thoughts and feelings. You will read more on how to be the best version of you, in Chapter 10 – Real Magic.

Here is a much simpler example. Imagine a group of five people going to a restaurant. As soon as they sit at a table and get the menus, each one of them has a different perception of what is happening in this experience we call a restaurant. One of them will look at the prices (reality focused on money). Another one will look at the dishes the restaurant serves (reality focused on the experience of the restaurant). Another one will look at the calories of the dishes (reality focused on health). Another one will look for only vegetarian dishes (reality focused on looking for his/her eating choices). And the last one will not look at the menu but will only look at the restaurant, seeing how loud or how pretty the restaurant is (reality focused on more external factors). They all have a different experience of the same reality.

I invite you to be open to the understanding that nothing really exists as you know it; everything is simply happening, and it is only through your perception of things (what you have inside) that you create your reality. Reality depends on the observer. Reality is just a concept based on what you decide to pay attention to, and on what you decide to observe.

Another way of looking at this is that your perception of the environment is what will create the outcome of your life. What you choose to look at, will create your thoughts and feelings. Life is an open mathematical equation, where the result of it depends on what you put into it. You are the one creating what goes into your equation, through your perception. Nothing is defined; open your mind to realize that the world you and I live in today—everything from "needing" a job to get money, to "needing" to live life a "certain way,"—is just a perception of life that you and I have assumed as truths, and are now our beliefs.

This is how you can start using your mind to create your new reality. You and I have been given a gift. You and I have been given the gift to shape our reality based on our perception of things. You can decide and train yourself to see what you want to see. No matter what the environment or circumstances are, whether they seem to be good or bad, remember that things simply *are*. You are the one that, through your perception, gives any experience any meaning.

Perhaps something "bad" that's happening to you is simply happening to help you understand what you truly desire in life. That circumstance is here to help you know what you don't like so that you can focus on what you like. Yet most of the time, you cannot see beyond what's happening in that moment. What's happening to you, is happening for you. Again, nothing has meaning in this life until you give it one. You can choose to perceive any experience that simply happens (whether it is *"good"* or *"bad")* as messages of love. Choose to see everything as a message for you, so that you can define what you like and what you do not like. Nothing happens to you; everything happens for you.

The concept of perception is key to understanding this world of illusions. You are even using your perception while reading this book. How you decide to subjectively interpret the information you are reading will change the way you are looking at this information. As one of my favourite authors put it:

"When you change the way you look at things,
the things you look at change."
– **Wayne Dyer**

Chapter 6

The Magic of Quantum Physics

Quantum Physics 101

I am by no means an expert in quantum physics; nor do I have a PhD at all. But I am fascinated by this subject and how, through researching and studying it, it is clear to me that the basics of quantum physics are essential to the subject of manifestation, living the dream life you desire, and creating and experiencing miracles in your life.

The easiest way to describe quantum physics is to talk about Albert Einstein's theory of relativity. Part of the theory of relativity talks about the electrons, the main particles that create reality and what everything is made of. Albert Einstein said that the electrons behave relative to the observer; energy becomes matter, and it all depends on the observer and his or her perception of what he or she observes—the theory of relativity.

When scientists observed the electrons, they were not able to find a *physical thing*. They realized that the electron existed as an **energy-wave**. Whenever they had the **intention** to truly see the electron, they observed that the electron changed from **energy-wave** into a **particle** (matter). The electron went from energy-wave and collapsed into particle (matter), at the precise point in space they chose to observe. This is fascinating; it is mind blowing! But what does this mean? This means that you control your reality; it means that you create your own reality. It means that whatever you *observe* (the pictures in your head) becomes **matter**. It means that whatever you put your attention on, goes from energy-wave and becomes particles (matter).

Let's dig deeper. If everything is energy, how are you able to see it? The reason you can *see energy* as a physical thing, is because once the electron goes from wave into matter, it emits a photon. A photon is a fundamental particle of light that makes everything we see in this physical world visible. So, if your *observation* (in your imagination) is a house—let's say it's your dream house for example—you are starting to collapse energy-waves into particles. The more you imagine this dream house, the more you keep collapsing electrons from waves into particles. Then these electrons start to emit photons, and all of a sudden the house appears in your reality—you simply bump into it. You can now see this house in your life experience because, remember, when the electrons emit photons, you are now able to actually see the house in your reality. This not only applies to your dream house, but it also applies to everything you can possibly imagine or think: love, abundance, financial situations, whatever you want—your life project.

You create your reality by *observing* and *collapsing* energy waves into particles. You create your reality by observing mental pictures of what you want (or what you DON'T want), in your imagination.

So how could you and I apply this principle of quantum physics to create anything we want in our lives?

The answer is, through pictures. You create your reality by images, through your imagination. The images in our minds are like little movies of either what we want or what we do not want. The problem is that most people, and this might be happening to you too, spend most of their time thinking about and imagining what they don't want. You can easily see people always talking or complaining about the weather or something that happened on the news, or complaining about how busy work and life is, or how projects are not going well, or the pain they feel in their bodies, etc.

From now on, be aware and create the consciousness to only talk about dreams, happy endings, and positive possibilities. Remember, the Quantum Field (this Source Energy) is always responding to your imagination, to the pictures you observe in your mind's eye.

Imagination creates reality. And remember, you can only imagine good things if you are conscious and aware of what is going on in your mind. Be aware of the pictures you decide to put in your mind. Are you making the effort to think of the images related to your dream life and the desires you want to experience in your life? Or are you still running old *scary movies* of what you don't want to experience? And are you still choosing to complain about things, talk about pains, and to be angry, stressed, or anxious?

These are the basics of how to collapse energy waves into particles, and how to create things from the invisible into the visible. Remember, everything in this Universe is made out of energy. Everything in this Universe is made of electrons.

Electrons are made out of energy. Your thoughts are energy. Your feelings are energy. Your imagination is energy. Everything you can imagine exists in energy-waves that you can collapse into particles (matter). You and I have the power to collapse waves into particles; everyone has this power. We are all quantum humans!

Happy imagining!

The Universe Is Always Saying "YES"

The Universe is always saying "yes." It's one of those universal laws that applies to you, whether you like it or not, and whether you are aware of it or not. The Universe is always saying "yes."

This is extremely important to carry with you as you go about your life. Please do not take this lightly. It's one of the most powerful tools you can ever be aware of. It has changed my life forever. We will see later, in Chapter 8 – Understanding Real Magic, how this Universe has your back, how this Universe wants you to live, and how you have the power of this Universe running through you. But for now, please be aware of the fact that this Universe is always saying "yes" to whatever you put out there. Go ahead; try this right now:

You: "My job sucks; I hate it…"
A: The Universe says: "YES"
You: "My job is great; I love what I do…"
A: The Universe says: "YES"

You: "I can't lose weight…"
A: The Universe says: "YES"
You: "Losing weight is totally possible."
A: The Universe says: "YES"

You: "Agh! I am so dumb!" (Whenever you make a mistake, you might tend to react by saying something like this.)
A: The Universe says: "YES"
You: "I am brilliant!"
A: The Universe says: "YES"

You: "I am not good at this..."
A: The Universe says: "YES"
You: "I can do this..."
A: The Universe says: "YES"

You: "I think I screwed this one up…"
A: The Universe says: "YES"
You: "Everything is going to be OK."
A: The Universe says: "YES"

You: "Do I look fat in these jeans?"
A: The Universe says: "YES"
You: "I am beautiful. I am powerful. I am happy. I am…"
A: The Universe says: "YES"

The power and the energy of the Universe is like water. If you water your garden, water doesn't choose which plants grow and which ones don't. It doesn't choose weeds over roses; it simply doesn't know how to choose. Water simply gives life to both, equally; it helps both roses and weeds grow. The Universe is the same; it nurtures and responds to whatever you are paying attention to. It will make your thoughts, ideas, and beliefs grow; it will make them a reality. The Universe only knows how to nurture and grow whatever seed YOU decide to plant. The Universe doesn't distinguish between good or bad because there is no good or bad in this Universe; there is only what you pay attention to.

You and I were given free will in order to exercise this connection to the Universe. We came into this life knowing that we are supposed to have fun with this principle, but somewhere along the way, we have forgotten about this power. So, from now on, please remember this powerful principle: The Universe is always saying "yes."

It is very important to always be aware of the internal dialogue you have with yourself. Make the little voice that keeps telling you what you think you can or cannot do, have the correct dialogue. Yes, you can do and be anything and everything you desire. Start by practicing this little but huge exercise with your inner self. Whatever you are paying attention to and thinking about, the Universe is always saying "YES" to it. The Universe is nurturing those thoughts and feelings, making them grow and making them your reality.

Chapter 7

Physical Senses vs. Spiritual Senses

Never Trust Your Physical Senses

I gave this chapter a lot of thought. I didn't know how to tackle it, but hopefully I found a way to get the message across. I truly believe in what you are about to read, especially the second part, your spiritual senses. But first, let's talk about the five physical senses and how, perhaps, we should all stop relying so much on them.

Your five physical senses (sight, hearing, touch, smell, and taste) are always *lying* to you. Let's take a look at how this happens in a simple magic trick:

When I perform a magic trick, the only way I can misdirect my audience's attention, or in other words, fool them, is because I understand how much they rely on their five senses (yep, this includes you too). I use your five senses to distract you from what's really happening. I especially focus on your sight, touch, and hearing to accomplish an illusion. Let me explain this further.

Let's say that I'm performing a simple card trick. First, I will ask you to shuffle the cards. By giving you the cards and letting you shuffle them, I'm appealing to your sense of touch and sight. I am giving you a false illusion that you are in control. I am creating the feeling, through those two senses, that there is no possible way I could know the order of the cards; which I don't, but by you shuffling the cards, you are convincing yourself that you have more control of the situation than me. You choose a card; I then ask you to put it back into the deck of cards, somewhere in the middle, and I give the cards yet another shuffle. The way I shuffle the cards might look like I'm completely unaware of where your card could possibly be. I am appealing to your sense of sight. Now I have two of your strongest senses on my side: sight and touch.

At this point, it is too late. By now, I already know where the card is, and what the card is. By the way, I've also appealed to your sense of hearing when I was shuffling the cards. You are not only seeing the cards being shuffled, you are also hearing them being shuffled. Now, this illusion is very convincing. And to top it all, I now ask you if you would like to shuffle the cards one more time. Most likely, you'll say yes, because you don't trust me, and you want to make sure you are in control. But again, it is a little too late; I've accomplished the art of using your own senses against you to deceive your brain.

I just described what happens during a simple card trick. I just described an environment created between two people. Now, let's take a look at how this happens in a more complex environment—life.

You and I were given our five physical senses to interpret and experience the physical world around us. But perhaps you and I might be depending too much on the five physical senses. You might be using them for more than just experiencing this physical world; you might be relying on them to create your reality instead of just experiencing it.

Let's take a look at a very simple example of how your five physical senses are fooling you all the time. Right now, if you're standing still, sitting down, or lying down, your five senses are giving you the illusion that you are not moving. But you and I know that this is not true; you and I are always moving, aren't we? Earth is in constant rotation. You and I are always moving with it, yet our senses deceive us into believing that we're standing still. They have created the illusion that you are in a single point in time, and space is sitting still. This same illusion happens when you are inside a moving car; it truly feels like you are not moving, even though you might be driving at 100km/hr.

I would like you to be open to the idea that our five physical senses are given to us only to interact and experience this physical world. Be open to the idea that you and I rely too much on the information we *experience* through these physical senses; we accept this information as truths instead of as just experiences. Through our five senses, we make experiences personal; but they are not personal—they are simply experiences.

Try to imagine your physical senses only as tools to experience the part of you that is physical, the human part of you, this *case* you call your body; and especially don't allow what you **see** and what you **hear** to become what you accept as real. Everything you experience on the outside is a reflection of the inside. Your physical senses are limited by nature, but don't worry though; it's a good thing that we also have our *spiritual senses.*

Your Spiritual Senses

What you are about to read is something I've been thinking about for quite a while now. The following is something that came to me as a revelation. My intention is that by sharing this with you, you are open to the possibility that there is something interesting and true about what you are about to read. This makes a lot of sense to me, and I hope it touches on a thing or two that you feel is true as well...

There are other types of senses you should be aware of, senses that you and I should be re-learning how to use, and how to make them stronger and more sensitive. These senses are essential for you to create and manifest anything you want. I call them *the spiritual senses*. These are the *real* ones, the ones you should be using to create anything and everything in your life. These spiritual senses are inside of you, and the only way to get to experience them and activate them is by eliminating some, or most, of the physical ones.

Here is how to first eliminate your physical senses so that you can tap into your spiritual ones.

Find a quiet place. Sit down on a chair, or on the floor, or you could even lie down flat. Close your eyes and keep them closed. By closing your eyes, you have now eliminated your most influential physical sense—your sight. You should also try to wear headphones and play some kind of soft, ambient, soothing music—nothing with lyrics or hard noises—something smooth and relaxing, like theta or alpha sound waves. By doing this, you have now eliminated any noise from your environment that might be distracting, like squeaky noises in your house, cars in the street, or any noise that could distract your attention away from this present moment. You have now eliminated your second most influential physical sense—hearing. And of course, if you are not eating, or smelling anything, or touching anything, you have now eliminated all of your five physical senses. All that is left is that blackness behind your eyelids. You are left with what's inside your mind's eye. This is how you start entering this world of energy. This is how you start connecting with the deeper Energy Love Force inside of you, and all its unlimited power. Hang on though, this is just the beginning. I will talk more about what to do once you close your eyes, in Chapter 9 – The Habit of Magic.

We are all born with these spiritual senses that I was previously talking about; we just don't really know how to use them, or even know that they exist. We were never taught how to create a connection to them. But from time to time, we actually do use them. It is more of a happy accident, as you and I were not aware that they existed before. These spiritual senses are the ones helping us make good decisions in our lives. They help us feel at peace; they help us experience happiness and joy. They are the ones we tap into when we have a "gut feeling" that leads us to the right choice. It is that inner, peaceful (not fearful) voice you sometimes listen to that seeks the path to love, happiness, peace, and joy.

Now let's take a look at what they are, and how to use them.

Awareness

This is the sense that starts and activates it all. Without starting to master this sense, you wouldn't be able to get into experiencing the rest. Awareness is the key to starting your journey into understanding who you truly are, and how to create magic in your life.

So, what is awareness? Awareness is knowing what your thoughts, feelings, and actions are all the time. It is knowing what your current *state of being* is all the time. It is looking at the bigger picture of what is happening right now, all the time. It is detaching yourself from the physical world, and understanding that everything around you is energy, vibration, and frequency. Awareness is the constant questioning of: "How am I feeling right now? What are my thoughts right now? What am I putting my attention on?"

We have previously talked about this, but you are only aware of 5% of your thoughts. The rest is a subconscious program you have installed over the years. So, being aware of your thoughts and feelings is going to be a constant battle and training. But how do you know if you have been able to regain and retain your awareness? The goal is to be constantly understanding and knowing what you think about most of the time.

Here are a couple of exercises you can do to practice awareness:

Number one –
Ask yourself these two questions, multiple times, throughout the day. Perhaps you can write them on a Post-it note, and carry it with you all the time:

- How am I feeling right now?
- What am I thinking about right now?

Ask yourself these questions at least every half hour. Answer these questions with pure honesty. There are no judgements. No one is watching; this is between you and you only. If you forget to ask these questions on a constant basis, then you are not being aware of your thoughts and feelings. Therefore, your awareness level is low. And it's easy for you to fall into a zombie mode that keeps you on autopilot 95% of the day.

Also, if the answer to those questions is that you are feeling stressed, anxious, angry, mad, sad, or afraid, or that you're thinking of what you need to do later on in the day, or you're thinking about what happened yesterday that bothered you, or you find yourself scrolling through your social media like a zombie, without any focus or intention, then your awareness is not being placed on the things that matter, nor is it in the present moment. Practice bringing your awareness into the present moment, and focus it on happiness, love, peace, and joy. Try to stay in this present moment for as long as you can. Then try again.

Energy-awareness

Energy-awareness is a deeper level of awareness, which I would encourage you to also start practicing. Energy awareness is the ability to feel the energy outside and inside of you. There are four streams of energy that you can become better at sensing.

The first one is the energy inside of you. Close your eyes and feel the energy inside of you. When you are truly connected to the awareness of the energy inside of you, you feel whole, you feel energized, you feel at peace, you feel warm, and you will feel a very strong sense of electricity and vibration of energy inside of you. Just close your eyes and start by feeling your heart beating. Keep your attention there and feel it; enjoy the warmth you feel once you find the beat.

The second one is the energy around your body. This energy expands when you feel happy, in love with life, and at peace; and it contracts when you are feeling sadness, frustration, anger, hate, and anxiety. You might have felt this energy around your body before. It feels like egg-shaped heat around you. You feel less heavy, and more like energy. You feel warm, and you can even feel the vibration, electricity, and heat around you. If you close your eyes and start imagining this energy flowing around you, with time, you will eventually start to feel it. It takes time, just like everything else you've learned in life. But I can promise you that once you start feeling this energy, it is one of the most comforting and peaceful feelings you will ever experience. It really helps if you imagine egg-shaped energy waves surrounding you.

The third one is the energy around other people, animals, places, and objects. You might already be aware of this, but sometimes you can feel someone else's energy when they enter a room. You might even sense when someone is happy or sad. You can sometimes feel energy emanating from someone without even looking at them.

The fourth one is sensing the energy that exists in the entire universe. This is a very wide concept, but there is only one energy connecting everything together—nature, humans, animals, places, objects—and we are all part of it. If you're able to close your eyes and start sensing that we are all connected through this one energy (because we are all made out of it), you are activating your energy-awareness and expanding it. Close your eyes, and try to imagine everyone connected to this one energy. Try to imagine the Universe and its infinity. We are all one.

Breathing

Breathing is a fundamental spiritual sense that you can use to reset your energy. In the action of taking a deep breath, holding it for a few seconds, and then letting it out, you are actually bringing all your energy back into your present moment. You cannot take a deep breath without being in the present moment; you have to focus in order to do so, and therefore you are bringing all of yourself into this moment.

Another word for breathing is respiration. The meaning of the word, *respiration*, is to *re-spirit*, or to spirit again. So, every single time you take a deep breath, you are gaining back your strength, and you are gaining back your spirit in the *now*. The word, *spirit*, can take a lot of different meanings, but essentially, *spirit* relates to the Power of Life, Creative Energy, your Energy Source, and the energy that created the world.

There is a reason why you and everyone else takes a deep breath right before you are about to do something big, something scary, or something incredible. The reason is that there is an intelligence inside of you that knows that through taking a deep breath, you are calling your spirit-energy back to you. Try to remember a very important or crucial moment in your life, perhaps a moment where you needed to feel courageous. By any chance, do you remember taking a deep breath seconds before you did whatever scary thing you had to do? Do you remember taking a deep breath and then getting that feeling of courage in that precise moment after taking that breath? This happens because, with every deep breath, you are calling your spirit-energy back to you—you *re-spirit*, and nothing can stop you.

Breathing allows us to regain our pure energy strength. It also helps us reconnect with Source Energy. That is why it is very important to practice your breathing and understand how it works.

Here is one exercise that can get you started on what to do:

Close your eyes. Take a slow breath in. Hold this breath in for a few seconds. Then let it out slowly. Do this for about three to five minutes every day when you wake up in the morning, and every night before you go to bed. Feel the air going in and out, focus on your heart, and have no thoughts. It's all about you in that moment.

Here is another exercise you can do as you get better with the exercise described above:

Focus your attention on your breathing. After a few deep breaths, start imagining a big ball of energy sitting at your pelvis area, just behind your reproductive organs. As you take a deep breath in, imagine sucking this ball of energy from your pelvis area up to your intestines, up to your stomach, up to your chest, up to your throat, up to your third eye (in between your eyebrows), and finishing on top of your head. All of this happens in one continuous, long and strong breath. This is a very active way of breathing. Your goal is to let the energy inside of you flow from the bottom of your body all the way to the top. Once you get to the top of your head, hold your breath for about five to ten seconds, and then release it. When releasing, relax your entire body; let go of everything. Do this for about ten times. Be patient; it gets better the more you do it. Remember, everything will take a little bit of time before you get a hold of it. Use your awareness to help you sense what's happening inside of you.

What you're trying to do by imagining energy moving from your lower pelvis area up to the top of your head, is to create a flow of energy; a flow of energy that has previously been stuck due to feeling stressed, anxious, afraid, sad, etc. Your *survival mode* stores energy in the lower part of your body, and you need that energy to flow in order to get to your *creative mode*, which starts in your heart. This is where manifestation begins.

Being Present

If you are not being present in the now, you are not connected to Source Love.

There is a lot of talk these days about living in the present moment. But what does that really mean? How can you truly achieve being present?

Being in the present moment requires a lot of practice and mastery. It is something everyone should be practicing all the time. It is the idea of forgetting anything that happened in the past (even seconds ago), and anything that could happen in the future. It is letting go of your identity, your name, gender, age, personality, situation, etc. It is forgetting about everything. If you are truly living in this present moment, you are *no-one, no-thing, no-body, no-place, and no-time*—you are a parent to no one; you are a sibling of no one; you are not a husband, a wife, a partner, a son, a daughter, etc. There is no time; there is no space. You are pure energy in this one eternal moment. You are simply an experience. Nothing and everything exists at the same time.

This concept of being in this one eternal moment is very important to understand. For example, let's say you are 33 years old. You are married and have one kid. Let's also say you have a sister, and your two parents live a couple blocks away from you. If you are truly in the present moment, it is as if you were born right in this very moment—imagine being born at 33 years old. You wouldn't know anything about this world. You wouldn't recognize your wife, siblings, or family. You wouldn't even know what being 33 years old even means. You wouldn't know your name or where you are or what language to speak. The only thing you would be aware of is the fact that you are pure consciousness and awareness. You would only be aware of the energy inside and around you. This is what it means to be in the present moment. It means that there is nothing but pure awareness and pure consciousness happening. You are simply happening.

How can you practice this?

Here is one way of doing this. Close your eyes, and focus on the energy that lives inside of you. *Feel* the energy inside of you. Focus your attention on just feeling energy inside and around you. Think about nothing for as long as you can (or focus your thoughts on feeling your heartbeat). If any thought comes to mind, you are not experiencing the present now. Take a deep breath and start again.

Remember this: When you are *feeling*, you are not *thinking* (your brain cannot pay attention to two things at the same time).

Silence

"I think 99 times and find nothing. I stop thinking, swim in silence, and the truth comes to me."
– Albert Einstein

Silence is the doorway to enter the spiritual world.

Silence is the answer to it all. Silence is the way. Silence helps you get clarity; it helps you find the answers you've been looking for. Peace is found in silence. Silence is friendly. Silence is kind. Silence is not the monster you think it is. It is full of love, happiness, peace, and joy. Find time to be in silence, and in *nothing* you will find *everything*.

You may have lost practice on how to be silent. Most people are not able to sit still for more than two minutes in silence without saying a word, yet alone without thinking any thought. The mastery of silence is something we all need to practice more, from speaking less to thinking less. By achieving inner silence, you are creating the space for *real magic* to come into your life; you are allowing miracles to flow in. Silence is the place where you will find peace.

Before any creation, there was silence. Think about this for a second: Before anything was created, there was silence. Before you say a word, there is silence. Before you think any thought, there is silence. Before you use your imagination, there is silence. Before there is movement, there is silence (being still). Before there was the galaxy as we know it, there was silence. Even before you came into this physical world, there was silence. Creation comes out of silence. This is why it is key to practice being in silence. Silence connects you to the inner part of you. That inner Energy Force, which is ready to create miracles in your life, can only be reached through silence. Don't be afraid of silence. Remember, in the other side of your busy mind, there is that peace you've been looking for.

Being in silence is turning off the little voice inside of you. Try doing this exercise: Close your eyes for one minute. Try to silence the voice inside of you. How long can you go before any thought pops into your mind? Five seconds? Ten seconds? Or perhaps you weren't able to find even one second of peace and silence before that voice kicked in. Are you thinking about what's for dinner? Are you thinking about the kids? Or are you thinking about *that* thing you need to do for work? My goal is to help you be aware of how connected or disconnected you are to silence. What's your relationship with this spiritual sense? Are you able to practice inner silence and not think about anything at all? Are you able to simply close your eyes and enjoy the feeling of silence?

Once you are able to silence all thoughts (eyes closed of course), feel the energy of silence, and stay there for a while (try a minimum of ten minutes). You will be able to get to a place where you will find peace. You will feel more rested by doing this for twenty minutes than sleeping for three hours. I can promise you that you will start to see things differently. You're going to stop rushing through life. You will start to connect more with the present moment. You will start to seek more silence, because now you know that peace is just a silent moment away.

Trust

In the next chapter, Chapter 8 – Understanding Real Magic, you will read about the concept that magic happens in the unknown. Magic and miracles happen in that uncertain area that we cannot predict. All I want to point out for now is that the unknown (where any magic happens) goes hand in hand with this spiritual sense of trust.

Trust is the one sense that requires you to conquer your fear of letting go, and your illusion of control (needing to control everything that happens in your life). You have to let go of the need to plan every single event that could happen in your life. When you simply *trust*, you're putting your awareness on the fact that life is perfect, that you are unlimited, that you are a Divine creator, and that everything works in your favor. You are acknowledging that there is this Divine flow of energy and love that is making this Universe work, and it is also taking care of you. Trusting this energy can only create more of the same experiences and feelings you are focusing on. By trusting that everything is OK, it is pulling miracles into your experience.

Before trusting completely, let me share with you the thinking behind why it's OK to simply trust and let go...

Humans created the concept of *duality*. Where there is good, we created bad. Where there is light, we created dark. Where there is happiness, we created sadness. And so on. Duality is just a concept created by our egos. Duality was created when humans felt *separation* from this Divine Energy. Duality was created the second humans forgot that we are part of this Divine Energy— we forgot that we are all one; we forgot that we are never alone; we forgot that our natural state of being is love, happiness, peace, and joy. Fear, anger, stress, anxiety, and hatred were born inside our heads; they are just ideas we created. They are ideas created out of fear, and ideas created out of the thinking that one day there is not going to be enough for you or for me. None of these negative concepts exist in the Spiritual Universe. The Spiritual Universe is unlimited, powerful, abundant, and infinite; and you are one with it.

There is no such thing as a *bad experience*. A *bad* experience is simply an experience. We are the ones that take what's happening and give it meaning. Most of the time, we choose to interpret experiences through fear, anger, lack, stress, and anxiety. If we can truly reconnect with who we really are, there is only happiness, love, peace, and joy. The Energy that created worlds is caring and loving. It is always creating more abundance. Just like nature, this Energy wants you to grow as much as you can. This Energy wants you to live as much as you can.

Think about this next thought for a moment:

If you experience a small cut on the palm of your hand, for example, the wound will eventually close up by itself. The wound will heal; this is just natural. This is what's supposed to happen. It is pretty magical that our body repairs itself. And if you truly let it, it can repair things beyond our comprehension. This Universe wants you to live! Life is always in perfect harmony if you allow it to be! The purpose of life is to always prosper and expand. This is a small example that could help you let go and start trusting; life is always working out for you. You live in a safe world; you live in this perfect place, at the perfect time, living the perfect experience for you at this moment. Simply trust that everything will work out for you, no matter what you're looking at right now.

Conquering trust is the most powerful connection you can develop with the Divine Energy that lives inside of you. You and I can get better at this.

Here is one exercise you can do: Every day, for the last five minutes before you go to bed, close your eyes and imagine yourself in a slow river. Imagine that this river represents the flow of life, the flow of the Divine Energy in you. Start to feel that your life, and all the experiences in it, are exactly where they need to be. Everything around you is exactly how it's supposed to be. Everything is in the right place and in the right time. Imagine that you are letting go of any limited perception of whether something is good or bad. Once you are in this river, simply let go, and just go with the flow; nothing else matters. Relax. Imagine yourself floating down this river of trust. Feel that you are part of this big flow of energy that is only working for your best life experience.

"To have faith is to trust yourself to the water. When you swim, you don't grab hold of the water, because if you do, you will sink and drown. Instead, you relax and float."
– Alan Watts

Imagination

"Imagination is more important than knowledge."
– Albert Einstein

Imagination is very powerful. It's pure manifestation. This spiritual sense is half in the Spiritual Universe and half in the Physical Universe.

I want you to imagine something you truly desire. Perhaps it is something related to health or wealth, or something material, or something non-physical—an experience. Do you have a clear mental picture of that desire? Good! I would like you to be aware of the following: The thought of your desire was not present in your head seconds before I asked you to imagine it. It didn't exist in your head before I asked you to put your attention on it. This thought existed outside of you, in the Spiritual Universe, in the Invisible World. And by using your imagination, you *captured* this thought, and brought it into your mind's eye. Imagination is like a net that catches all thoughts; all thoughts already exist as a possibility in the Quantum Field or Spiritual Universe.

Anything and everything you can possibly imagine, think about, or experience in your life, is somewhere out there—it already exists. For example, imagine a version of you that has everything you've ever desired and wanted. If you are able to imagine this scenario, it means that this version of you already exists as a possibility in the Quantum Field, and through your imagination, you are able to catch that thought. You are literally manifesting a thought that was not present inside of your head a second ago.

In order to become that *version of you*, the one who is already experiencing those desires, you must *be* that version **right now**. By using your imagination, you can start being rich, healthy, free, unlimited, etc., right now. If you live your life through your imagination, feeling like this *version of you* is already you, the facts (your environment) will eventually catch up with the truth (the true self that you are picturing to be). This is why thinking positively doesn't work—because you don't attract what you think about; you attract more of what you already are. And by using your imagination, you can live in your vision of who you *truly are*—this perfect version of you. You have to live your life as if what you desire has already happened.

"Don't think of what you want. Think from what you want."
– Neville Goddard

You have to practice having no boundaries, while imagining anything. The sky is not the limit; there is so much more. Take the time to truly shape and imagine your perfect life, and start living in it, inside your head. Imagination is the key to defining your path. Have you ever truly spent more than ten minutes imagining what your perfect life looks like? Have you crafted that thought? How does it feel? What do you do when you wake up in this amazing dream life? What do you eat? Who are you with? What time of the day is it? Where are you? What's the weather like? What type of activities do you do? What type of thoughts does this person (you) have? How does this person react to others?

Everything in this Visible World started in the Invisible World. Everything you can see, touch, and experience started in someone's imagination; your phone, your computer, and even you started as a thought in someone else's imagination. So, if you want to create something new, you have to go into that Invisible World—the Spiritual World, the Quantum Field.

Play with your imagination. Become a master of using it. You have to imagine your desires as though they've already happened; believe they are real, and they will. Convince yourself that they are real, and so they will be. That's how hard you have to imagine your perfect life.

Remember, either *you are* or *you are not*. There is no such thing as *becoming*.

So, if your current reality is showing you information that you are *not* living your desires and your dreamed life, you have to ignore the illusion you are perceiving. This is how you change your reality. You can live your dream life right now. As an incredible mentor once told me:

"The facts (your environment, the physical evidence, the experiences around you) will catch up with the truth (who you choose to be inside)."
– James MacNeil

Intention

Intention is your desire in action. Once you define a clear vision of what you desire to manifest (what it is, how it looks, how it feels to experience it, etc.), your intention is every single action you do, think of doing, or take toward making that desire happen.

Let's take losing weight as an example. Living a healthy life, which reflects a strong and fit body, is your intention. Any thought, feeling, or action toward this vision of yours, such as buying that gym membership, looking up healthy recipes, drinking more water, feeling beautiful and powerful, etc., is your desire in action. Your desire is activating your inner self, your inner energy, to do or think all of these thoughts, feelings, or actions through that clear intention. Whether you actually accomplish all of these goals or not, in the beginning, it doesn't matter. Your intention has started a snowball effect inside of you that wasn't there before. This is the power of intention. Your intention is connected to Source Energy. When you allow it, your intention takes a life of its own. This is how you connect to the Spiritual World through your intention; you simply allow it to take a life of its own. And as long as you have clearly defined it, nothing and no one will stop you from getting there, not even yourself. The key is to create the habit of revisiting your intention every moment of the day. If you stay connected to your intention, you start living from it. You start experiencing it inside of you; eventually, it becomes present outside of you.

After defining a clear intention, you must place this intention in two places: in your heart and in your mind's eye (behind your eyes and in between your eyebrows). Imagine that you literally put a ball of energy, representing your desire, inside your heart and inside your mind's eye. Once you embrace that intention and visually place it inside these two places, it's quite interesting to notice how everything you do will start to gravitate toward this dream of yours. And if you keep reminding yourself that you have now anchored your clear intention inside these two places, once you touch either your heart or your head, it will become easier to live from that new state of being—that desire.

Every morning and every night, you must define a clear intention for the day and for the night. For example, "It is my intention to enjoy every moment of today." "It is my intention to be aware of my thoughts at all time." "It is my intention to live a prosperous and abundant life." Or at night, "It is my intention to have a great rest so that my body and mind can regenerate and heal," etc. Your body and brain will start listening to your clear intentions. Remember, a clear-formed intention comes from the *spiritual you*; it is full of love and peace. And maintaining the elevated emotions and feeling as if your desire (your intention) has already happened, will make the experience come to you.

Intuition

Intuition is the little voice that guides you in those hard moments when you don't seem to know what to do. When you get quiet, when you silence your thoughts and stop thinking, you will all of a sudden see clarity, and the answer will come to you— that is how to connect to your intuition.

Your intuition pushes you to greatness. It never comes from a place of fear; it only knows love and peace. Your intuition can never guide you wrong. Your intuition will always have the answer to that problem.

It's very important not to confuse the voice of your intuition with the voice of the ego—fear. Ego's voice will always come from a place of separation; ego's voice will be full of anger, fear, anxiety, or sadness. Your intuition will always feel right. When you listen to your intuition, you always know what the right thing is to do; it always knows that everything is going to be OK.

Your intuition is a connection to your spirituality. It's the internal dialogue between Divine Energy and the Divine You. You might have experienced something like the following: Have you ever felt the need to call or contact someone? Have you ever felt like taking a different way home? Have you ever felt the need to talk to that stranger you saw on the street? Have you ever felt the need to help a person you have never seen before? In all of these scenarios, your intuition is talking to you. Whenever you feel the need to do something out of the ordinary, or to try something new, perhaps something that might seem scary or something that you might not normally do, be aware that it is your intuition talking to you.

In order to listen to what your intuition is trying to tell you, you must get silent. The answer will always come to you. Your intuition is always in touch with the Source Energy; it is part of it, and it is part of you. Your intuition comes from a place of love and peace; it has infinite wisdom, and it is always one silent moment away.

Purpose

Purpose is a very interesting spiritual sense to understand. It is a spiritual sense (as well as the others) that creates a connection to the Spiritual Universe. Purpose can only be experienced; it can only be felt, and it can only be lived in this present moment.

Your entire life, you have been conditioned to believe that you need to find your life's purpose out there. You have been told to look for it somewhere on the outside, or perhaps you have felt that you needed to figure out the reason you are on this planet. This is where I think we have been misguided or have built an incorrect belief about our life's purpose.

Your life's purpose will never be found on the outside. It is not out there; you do not need to go and find it. Your life's purpose is already inside of you—and yes, you do have one. By the mere fact that you are alive right now, and that you were born into this world, you have a purpose. Your purpose is not hiding from you at all, and it is not a problem you need to solve.

Your life's purpose will not come to you through thinking about it, and it will not come to you through your thoughts. Your life's purpose can only be experienced when you live in the present moment, when you are aware, and when you are conscious. It can only be experienced through your heart. It can only be experienced when you are doing what you love; you need to do what inspires you.

Purpose is peace. And when you discover your life's purpose through being present in everything you do, it will take a life of its own. You will discover a greater you, someone you didn't know existed.

Don't go searching for your life's purpose; you will miss out on life. Get quiet, and let it come through you by always being present. Don't rush it.

I can definitely assure you that you have felt your life's purpose a few times throughout your life. You have had the feeling that you were in the right place, at the right time, helping someone, inspiring, doing something that you love doing, talking passionately about something you love, losing track of time, enjoying yourself, feeling creative, and being passionate, full of energy, etc. You must keep playing. Your life's purpose is somewhere inside of you; listen to it, keep connecting to it, and don't only experience it a few times—start living through it.

Chapter 8

Understanding Real Magic

The Magic Outside of You
(the Magic That Creates Worlds)

The world we live in is such a beautiful place, full of miracles. It is full of different colours, smells, shapes, weather, etc. Take time to pay attention to nature all around you; there are so many answers you can find and feel, just by looking at nature. For example, how tall does a tree grow? Answer: As tall as it can, as much as it can! It actually never stops growing. By nature, trees and plants are designed to keep growing and expanding. You and I are also designed to keep growing and expanding. Humans are the only species that by choice, don't grow to their full potential. Humans are the only species that looks for a comfort zone and decides to stay there. It is incredible to realize that by choice, we decide to stop our own growth, and we do not tap into our full potential. And this choice has now become a habit. Remember Chapter 3 – The Power of the Brain? But let's get back to the magic outside of you.

Open your awareness to the whole picture of the entire planet Earth. This planet has oceans, volcanoes, forests, deserts, mountains, jungles, etc.—so many environments and ecosystems working in perfect harmony for the greater life of this planet. The most amazing part of it all is that *nothing falls out of place*: Oceans don't start to float into space; trees don't stop producing the oxygen we breathe; the atmosphere provides the perfect ecosystem in which we can survive, etc. There is an Energy Force that keeps everything in place, working in perfect harmony. There is a Love Force that keeps water in place, mountains tall, forests breathing, deserts hot, and jungles humid—a perfect ecosystem.

Now let's take a look at an even bigger picture. This Energy Force is also the same Love Force that keeps our planet rotating in a perfect orbit around the sun. It is the same Energy Force that keeps all planets moving in perfect harmony; planets don't fall out of their orbit. Again, there is something incredible holding it all together, a Divine Intelligence, that just keeps things in place. This Divine Intelligence keeps everything moving how it's supposed to. It keeps the sun warm and the Universe moving. This glue that keeps everything together is Pure Love.

This is the *magic* outside of you. It is everywhere; it is in the entire Universe—it is the Universe, an Energy Love Force that only knows harmony and love. And if you are able to close your eyes and feel how everything is in the right place, being held together by this Energy Force, you are allowing yourself to connect to this Energy and attract more of that power into your life.

Guess what? This Energy Force lives inside of you too. The same energy that created worlds, lives inside of you. The same energy that is keeping this entire Universe in place, lives inside of you. The same energy that moves a shooting star across the galaxy, moves a thought inside in your head. The same energy that keeps the sun warm, keeps your heart beating. And you can tap into this giant Energy Force to create anything you want in your life. You just have to become aware of it. And by becoming aware of it, understanding that you are powerful by nature, you are honouring your worthiness to receive miracles in your life, and to create them. You stop becoming a victim of your circumstances, and you start being the creator of your environment. You start understanding that things don't happen to you, and that things happen for you and because of you. You are an extension of this Energy. You are an extension of this Universe. And it is only until you understand your connection to this Divine Intelligence that you will be able to claim your power and create the world you want—your world.

The Magic Inside of You

It took me a long time to understand and live my life from this simple truth: There is magic living inside each and every single one of us. It's one of those things that I took for granted. I knew it was there, yet I didn't really know it was there or how it got there, or what to do with it. It's just hard to see the bigger picture when you are not paying attention to it.

Let me share with you some of the thoughts and feelings I found to be incredibly eye-opening. The following are thoughts and feelings that I constantly repeat in my head every day, to remind myself how lucky and fortunate I am to be right here and right now. Understanding and repeating the following thoughts, and the feelings that accompany these thoughts, will start creating new neuro-patterns in your brain. These new neuro-patterns will eventually start to replace old harmful habits, like complaining or placing your attention on what's bothering you. The more you think about these new magical thoughts, the more you will destroy old harmful ones.

While reading this next paragraph, please try to follow along with the energy of your emotions (energy in motion). Allow yourself to fully embrace what you are about to read. Imagine and feel what I am about to walk you through. You should practice this exercise every day and every night. It only takes about five minutes to complete, yet when truly engaged, the results will help you stay connected to the Source Energy that will create miracles in your life. So please, open your focus and keep your attention on what I am about to say, and you will feel the abundant, powerful, and magical Love Force that keeps it all together. Do this on a regular basis, create a habit out of this routine, and you will create more of the *same* in your life.

The *magic-inside-of-you* meditation –

Become aware of your heart beating. Think about the following: Are you the one giving your heart the instructions of how it should beat? Or is your heart beating by itself, just because it *knows* how to? Become aware of the fact that it is not you, consciously, who controls your heart's beat. Your heart is beautifully beating without you telling it when and how to do it—this is real magic.

Now become aware of your lungs. Pay attention to how air comes in and goes out. It's not until you pay attention to them that you become aware of how your lungs do this miraculous function. Again, you are not willingly commanding your lungs to do the function; they already *know* what to do. They simply take the right amount of air that your body needs to live, and they exhale just the right amount of carbon dioxide that your body needs to get rid of. Become aware of the fact that it is not you, consciously, who controls taking what you need from the air and getting rid of what you don't need—this is real magic.

The same happens with every single function of your body: the blood traveling in your body; the way your digestive system takes the food you eat, processes what it needs, and gets rid of what it doesn't. Become aware of the incredible bodily functions that you do not have to think about—but most importantly, have no control over—yet they are all work in perfect harmony, keeping you alive. The most important thought you should be aware of is the fact that you are not controlling any of these. You are just a host to all of these **miracles**; you are a host to this Love Force that keeps everything *glued together*. You are a host to **real magic**.

Keep your attention and your awareness on the incredible feeling that there's something inexplicable inside of you that just wants you to exist. Feel this incredible energy that creates all of what is you, coordinating the trillion cells in your body to operate with synchronicity just for you to exist. Feel this energy. Make a conscious effort, and imagine that the same energy that keeps this Universe alive (planets, the sun, galaxies, stars, oceans, trees, sky, etc.) is the same energy that keeps you alive. Keep your attention on this energy and the feeling of it for as long as you can.

Practice this connection.

End of Meditation.

There is an incredible and powerful energy inside of you keeping everything together, something working in perfect harmony for you to exist. There are so many miracles already happening inside of you—this is the magic inside of you.

Science has given this *magic* a name: the autonomic nervous system. But if you really think about it (putting that name aside), there is something miraculous living inside of you. This energy is always working in your favor. This energy wants your life to exist, prosper, and go on. This Divine Energy or Divine Intelligence simply makes everything work perfectly. It is the same magic that created mountains and oceans. Creation is the only purpose of this magical energy. And by getting out of your own way (by not thinking about your past, your future, or any circumstances that might be making you feel stress and anxiety), you are allowing this Divine Intelligence to do what it does best: create magic in your life. Focus your attention on it by just being aware of it. Practice the *magic-inside-of-you* meditation, and start feeling miracles in your life.

You could also use the meditation above for healing. I am discovering how to apply this in my life in order to heal certain parts of my body. I am truly convinced that this Divine Energy heals; it has the power to do so. It is the same Divine Intelligence that creates new cells in your body when you have a small cut on your hand or your knee. This Divine Intelligence is pure love and pure power. This Divine Energy does not care if it is a small paper cut or a very aggressive disease. This Divine Intelligence is unlimited and infinite; it makes no difference to it. It only knows how to create and how to give life, and it just wants you to live. When truly connected, when you get out of your own way, this Divine Energy takes over and returns your body to its natural state of being—perfect health.

What you just read in the previous paragraph is true. There are multiple people in this world who are experiencing miraculous healings in their lives. So, why not be open to this happening to you, whatever you are going through. Simply close your eyes and imagine that this Divine Energy, this magic, is doing what it does best, and *feel* it inside your body. Become aware of the magic *inside of you*, and once you are there, call to yourself feelings of love, health, peace, and harmony. Be thankful for not really understanding how this energy works (you don't have to understand how it works); just be grateful for knowing that it works, and that it's there. Let go of any need to control the situation. Let go of any judgement; let go of any fears. Stop trying to reason with your limiting beliefs of why this would or wouldn't work for you. Just *feel* how everything inside of you is working perfectly for you.

When you do this, you are now causing an effect inside of you. You are being a creator of life, not a victim of destiny. Do this, and you will attract more wonderful experiences of health, abundance, harmony, love, and peace. Honour this magical state of being, over and over again, every day. Take ten minutes in the morning and ten minutes at night; you can even do this while riding the train, or while showering. If you truly give it a shot, you will see changes in your energy and in your life. I know I did. You cannot change your life unless you change your energy. Just keep practicing your connection to this inner magic, and watch everything around you start to change. Start to see how the magic inside of you starts to create magic outside of you.

The Magic of Being Connected to Source

Being connected to this Divine Energy is the only way you can create and experience magic in your life. When you are connected, you feel at peace; you feel at home. Being connected to this Energy Source is what's natural, yet it's not normal these days. People choose to live in *survival mode*. The good news is that at different points throughout your life, you've already been connected to this Energy Force; you just didn't know that you were connected to it.

When you are in *creative mode*, you are connected to the Divine Intelligence. When you are inspired, you are connected to the Divine Intelligence; and this is what I really want to talk about—being inspired.

There is so much power behind being inspired. To be inspired means to be *in-spirit*; it means to be in a place of creation. When you are *in-spirit*, you are in your natural state of being—you are a creator. Let's take a musician; for example, a piano player. Have you noticed that when a musician is playing his/her instrument, whenever they play that cool *solo*, their eyes are closed? It looks like they are somewhere else. To us, the viewers, it looks like they are *glowing*; to us, it looks beautiful, and it looks powerful. This is because they are inspired; they are *in-spirit*. Something bigger than all of us has taken over that artist. He or she is not in this Physical Universe; they are completely connected to Source. When anyone is doing something they truly love, they are inspired; and when they are inspired, they are connected to Source.

The same happens with any athlete out there. When athletes are in the middle of any game, they are not themselves. Something bigger than you, me, or them has taken over; this Divine Energy is now being channeled. You can ask anyone that has ever played sports and has had a perfect game, how they were able to accomplish such an amazing performance. Most of the time, they will say that they don't know how they did it; they simply felt unstoppable, and they simply felt that they couldn't miss—they simply felt "on fire."

I am very confident in saying that you have been *in-spirit* a few times throughout your life. You have for sure felt this connection to Energy Source. Perhaps you were more in touch with it when you were a kid, as all you had to do back then was to enjoy life (even though this is what you are supposed to be doing right now). This is why, as an adult, it is very important for you to keep on playing, to be playful, to practice your passions and continue doing what makes you happy.

And if you do not know what currently makes you happy, you are in a perfect position to start discovering what it is that inspires you. Is it dancing, cooking, running, exercising, painting, playing music, singing, writing, being in touch with nature, reading, baking, pottery, hiking, sailing, biking, swimming, yoga, performing magic, etc.? The more you are connected to this Divine Energy, the faster you will create and experience miracles in your life. Go find out what moves you, and do more of that which inspires you. Live in-spirit!

Magic Happens in the Unknown

The unknown could represent a very scary place for most people. Not knowing what could happen next is a feeling most humans are not familiar with, and try to avoid most of the time. I previously talked about the fear of letting go, and how perhaps you might not be used to the idea of living your life from a place of discovery, rather than from a place of planning ahead.

It is very important to understand one simple fact: Magic only happens in the unknown; miracles happen in the unknown. They cannot happen anywhere else. So, you must learn how to let go of this sense of control. You must learn how to live from a place where there are no judgements; a place where fear is not an option, only trust. You must learn how to be comfortable with not knowing what could happen tomorrow or the next hour or the next second. You must learn how to live life in the unknown. Let me say this one more time: **Magic (miracles) only happens in the unknown.**

Imagine seeing a really good magic trick. Would you be amazed if you knew from the very beginning that the card you just chose and shuffled back into the deck was going to appear in my back pocket? Probably not. I just told you what to look for; I just told you how the trick ends before showing it to you. If you knew what's going to happen, there's no element of surprise; there is no magic. I cannot create the experience of magic without the unexpected factor. The same happens when someone is telling you a joke. If they tell you the end of the joke first, there is no joke.

The same applies to experiencing miracles in your life. Yes, they exist, and as a great mentor said:

"Those who believe in miracles, experience more of them."
– James MacNeil

If you knew when and how a miracle/magic was going to appear in your life, it wouldn't be called a miracle. It wouldn't feel like magic; it wouldn't be called a quantum leap. A joke is not funny without the element of surprise. A magic trick is not magical without the element of surprise. A miracle is not a miracle without the element of surprise. They all happen in the unknown.

Remember, there is an incredible Energy Force we are all part of, which exists outside and inside of us. We know that this Divine Intelligence is present everywhere, and that it is in everything in this Physical Universe, including the things and experiences we want to manifest into our lives. So, all you have to really do is to be aware of this Energy Force, and let it surprise you. Let this Source Energy show you real magic. The same way you simply are an observer enjoying a magic trick, be present in the now, and let yourself observe and enjoy magic in your life; be the observer of miracles. Miracles in your life will only happen in the unknown. Just align your intention (what you want) with your attention (your thoughts and feelings). That is your only job; the miracle part, trust me, is not up to you.

Start to see the unknown as your friend. It is where miracles live. The unknown is really excited to greet you with miracles, love, and presents. The unknown is waiting for you to embrace it, not fear it. You cannot experience a miracle if you don't let go of fear and the need to control. The unknown is like the *scary dog you were once afraid of:* Once you pet it for the first time, you realize that it is kind and playful, and it becomes your best friend. Learn to embrace something so wonderful and full of infinite possibilities. The unknown is your friend. The unknown holds love, peace, and joy. The unknown holds everything you want to experience in your life.

Living in the Unknown

So, how do you live in the unknown? One of the questions you might be asking is: "How can I live in the unknown if I have to go to work at the same place, and see the same people, and do the same thing every day, over and over again?" Here is the answer: Even though it might seem like you are be going to the same places, which might give the illusion that you are doing the same thing, which gives the illusion that you are seeing the same people, etc., *nothing is ever the same.*

Nothing in this life can be the same. Energy is always in constant change and in constant expansion. Whether you are aware of it or not, energy is never static; it is always in motion. We are energy, our thoughts are energy, nature is energy, and things are energy. The only way anything can appear to be the same around you is because you have chosen to create the illusion of things appearing to be that way. Your subconscious program is trying to make your environment feel repetitive so that you can feel comfortable in it. Remember, nothing ever is or stays the same. Everything is always new. If you are able to constantly pull yourself into the present moment, the eternal now, everything is a new experience. Everything is experienced for the first time when you live in the present moment.

In Chapter 4 – Childlike Wonder, I talked about living in childlike wonder. I talked about how to live every single moment as if you have never experienced it before, because in reality, you haven't. Living in the *unknown* means understanding that you don't know where a conversation could lead to, or where any experience might take you. The more you start connecting with the energy of the now, the more you let go of the outcome that you have programmed your body to experience, and the more you let go of your fears, the more you start to see that nothing is the same. You start to see how this Divine Energy is communicating with you all the time. It is creating and unfolding your dreams and desires right in front of your eyes.

If you do not let yourself into the unknown, you won't be able to see the *messages*. The answers you are looking for can literally be right in front of you, yelling at you, and if you are not ready to see them, and if you are only worrying about what could be (fear), or if you are not aware of this Energy Force that only wants the best for you, the answers you are looking for will pass you by—you won't be able to see them.

If you practice living in the now, you understand that you do not know what could happen within the next ten seconds, and the next ten, and the following ten... There should be a feeling of excitement and anticipation running inside of you. You should start building the habit of feeling surprise and wonder for what could happen in your life. This will take time and practice, but you must work at reminding yourself, over and over again, that you truly do not know what could happen within seconds—and this is a great state of being to live in. You must create the *space* for surprises to come into your life. If you live a life where 95% of it is full of fears, what if's, stress, anxiety, schedules, plans, running from one place to another, anger, control, etc., then there is no room for surprises, miracles, serendipity, happiness, love, and magic. You might have successfully filled up your life with things you do not want. But it is never too late. You can always start to make room for the things you really desire to experience and bring into your life. Simply place your awareness (your energy) on trusting that everything is always working out for you. Place your attention on the concept of miracles, happiness, trust, love, and inner peace. Create the space within you for the unknown to come into your life, and let it do what it does best—real magic.

Here is an example of how you most likely already know how to live in the unknown but just forgot how to do it constantly:

Do you remember being a kid on Christmas morning? Do you remember how exciting it was to wake up early in the morning and run down the stairs to find a bunch of presents under the tree? I bet you couldn't sleep the night before. It was truly a magical moment. You were so excited to open those presents because, even though you didn't know what they were (the unknown), you knew for sure that there were going to be presents under the tree.

From now on, when you wake up every morning, simply think, "Today is Christmas!" Feel excitement and anticipation. Feel the thrill of living all the new experiences you are about to live in this new day *(opening the presents under the tree)*. Live with the joy of discovering the unexpected surprises you will find in every turn and every second of the day. Expect surprises and miracles in your day. You don't need to know what they are or how you are going to get them; you simply expect them to be there, and you go out there and discover them.

You must let go of your need to control; it is all fear. It is only fear of not knowing what lies ahead of you. Not knowing is OK. Living in the unknown will open infinite possibilities in your life. Don't be afraid. Everything is OK. You don't have to know how you are going to get the extra money you need. You don't need to know how you are supposed to get over something that is causing you emotional pain, bothering you, or making you anxious and stressed. Trust that magic will happen. Know that miracles are coming. Trust that the answers will appear. Trust in the unknown. Leaving room for what you don't know, will bring the answers, the surprises, and the gifts. Remember, everything is always working out for you.

Chapter 9

The Habit of Magic

The Magic of Your Thoughts

You might have not yet realized this, but thoughts are one of the most powerful forms of manifestation there is. Before a thought comes to you, *there is nothing.* Place your awareness on the fact that before any thought appears in your mind, this *thought* didn't exist; it wasn't there before. Therefore, we can say that from nothing, you created something—pure manifestation. By simply placing your attention and realizing what just happened, you are becoming more aware of the power you have to create anything and everything in your life. You are owning being a creator.

Throughout this book, I've previously mentioned that thoughts become things. If you take a certain thought, and you keep repeating it over and over again, this thought becomes a belief. Eventually, a belief becomes your personality, and your personality becomes your personal reality. So, if your personal reality doesn't look like what you want it to look like, it has to do with the fact that you are not paying close attention to the thoughts that you keep producing and repeating in your mind.

All creation starts from a thought. Everything in this Physical Universe first came into this world in the form of a thought that existed in the Spiritual Universe—from non-physical to physical, from invisible to visible, everything started as a thought.

Everything, from the smallest object to the greatest inventions of our modern days, started as a thought in someone's imagination. So, what thoughts do you keep repeating in your head? Thoughts become things.

In his book, *Becoming Supernatural*, Dr. Joe Dispenza mentions something absolutely incredible:

"Your body cannot tell the difference between an experience that happens outside of you (in the real world) and an experience created by thought alone (something you imagine)."

This is incredibly amazing and fascinating. This means that if you think about what you want, or about what you don't want, your body and every single cell inside of you believes that the experience is happening right now. This shows how powerful it is to think about what you want or to have any thought regarding happiness, love, joy, excitement, adventure, abundance, prosperity, etc. On the contrary, this also clearly shows how dangerous it is to have any thoughts regarding what you don't want to experience, or any thought regarding debt, sickness, stress, anxiety, accidents, old memories with any emotional pain, relationship break-ups, being fired, worrying, etc.

When you think about a negative scenario, or a negative past memory, your body will produce the corresponding chemical toxins and reactions as if the experience is happening right now. You are imprinting your cells with fear, stress, anxiety, and anger. You are teaching your body to remember these emotions, to make a habit of them; you are making these emotions part of your nature. This is how the body gets sick, and cells stop communicating with one another. This is also how the body can have a panic attack without you.

You have to stop mentally rehearsing, re-playing, or thinking about any worst-case scenarios; your body cannot tell the difference between a real experience and an experience created by thought alone. Your body cannot tell the difference between the past and the future.

On the contrary, if you can just close your eyes and mentally rehearse any scenario you truly want to experience—the best version of you, someone who is only pure love, peaceful, powerful, unlimited, joyful, creative, happy, almighty, healthy, wealthy, etc.—your body believes it is this person right now. If you imagine a version of yourself that is living in the perfect house, with the perfect partner, with the perfect career and the perfect life, etc.—if you invest your energy and feelings into crafting this thought—your body truly believes that it is happening right now. Your body will start to be that new self, right now. Your body even starts being that new self without you. And after doing this for a long period of time, after making the habit of your new self, the experience will find you. Now, this is real magic. This is how you start to pull your perfect life into the present now. This is how you simply decide to be who you truly want to be right now—simply imagine it, and mentally rehearse it, over and over and over again.

I am convinced that you know that what I talked about above is true. I'm sure you've had dreams that seemed so real that they felt as if you were there. I'm sure you've day-dreamed, or imagined things like getting a job, or nailing that interview, or you've imagined getting that first kiss, or any other scenario; and you've started to produce feelings and emotions (without knowing it) that got you really excited, as if the experience had already happened.

Your thoughts are so powerful that you can use them to create what you desire by teaching your body the feelings and emotions of that experience. The interesting thing here is that this applies for both positive and negative experiences. So, if you are able to focus your mind on creating the thoughts and the feelings related to the experiences you would like to manifest into your physical world, and if you are able to hold these thoughts and feelings long enough, your reality will change—it just has to. You are now reaching a higher level of consciousness, and your reality has to change based on this new level of consciousness. You stop being the old you, and you become the new you.

If you create a new life, and your body starts to already be that new life, then your old self will disappear; you cannot be two different people at the same time. And because now your body believes that the experiences that you have been mentally rehearsing have already happened, as if by magic, your *new dreamed life* will become your new personal reality. Your outside world will change, and the experience you first imagined will find you. That's right; what you desire will find you. This is the power of using your imagination. This is why it is so important to meditate, to focus your thoughts. This is why it is so important to close your eyes and mentally rehearse the best version of you. This is why it is so important to always be aware of the type of thoughts that are crossing your mind.

There are only two things happening in our minds at all times: We are either being defined by a limited thought of our past (fears, anxiety, stress, or anger), or we are being defined by a powerful vision of the future (happiness, love, peace, and joy).

Be a constant vigilante of your thoughts. Create this awareness. Use your thoughts as a tool to create and experience miracles in your life. Don't let any thought that isn't aligned with your dream life run around in your mind. Be a constant vigilante of any thought you put into your mind. Once you build a perfect version of you, or a perfect life, or a desire you really want to manifest, do not let anyone or anything divert you from living as if this thought had already happened. Remember, there will be people who will try to persuade you that what you are doing is nonsense, and that you should stop daydreaming; and one of those people trying to convince you to quit will probably be you. Use your thoughts for magic.

The Magic of Feelings

In the beginning of the book, I talked about how I felt like something was missing in my process of understanding the Law of Attraction. I felt like there had to be more than just thinking positively. Well, feelings were what I was failing to understand, and feelings are the most important element of manifestation.

Before we get into how to use feelings for manifestation, let's understand what feelings are, and where they come from.

I remember being in my first year of university. I was going through a tough break up. My mom kept telling me that I was feeling sad because I kept creating thoughts that reminded me about the break-up, and then those thoughts would create feelings of sadness and anxiety. She pointed out that I was focusing on thoughts of separation and fear; therefore, I was creating feelings of unhappiness. I was very upset at the fact that she wasn't able to understand that what I felt was different from what I thought. Little did I know, *Mom was right.*

But how is this possible? It didn't make sense that what I was feeling had to do with what I was thinking. I couldn't understand it at the time, but she was right—feelings come from thoughts. When you think a certain thought, that thought causes a certain feeling in your body, a feeling related to the thought you just had. That certain feeling in your body causes another thought, which will produce another similar feeling than the one before, and now you are trapped in this eternal thinking-and-feeling loop. It never ends unless you snap out of it and decide to transform that energy.

Another word for feelings is emotions. An emotion is energy in motion. That's what feelings are. Feelings are energy moving inside your body. And according to Einstein:

> **"Energy can never be created or destroyed; it can only be transformed."**

Therefore, if you're ever feeling sadness, anger, hatred, anxiety, depression, or fear, you cannot just get rid of those feelings and replace them with happiness, peace, love, or joy. You have to transform that energy. You have to go up the ladder of emotions until you get to happiness. And that transformation is just a decision away.

Here is an example of this ladder of emotions. If you are feeling some kind of depression, you must take depression and transform it into sadness. Then you must take sadness and transform it into *feeling neutral*. Then you must take *feeling neutral* and transform it into feeling just OK. From feeling OK, you must transform that energy into feeling better—from better to peace, from peace to joy, from joy to happiness, from happiness to being in love with life, and so on...

Changing how you feel is a process of transformation. Feelings are energy in motion. You cannot just get rid of one feeling and replace it with another. You must transform that energy.

This following thought is probably one of the biggest eye-openers of my entire life experience: Feelings are the language of the Universe; feelings are the language to manifest what you desire.

Feelings are the language of the Quantum Field. Feelings are the language of the Universe. Imagine that you are not able to ask for what you desire by using words, or thoughts (because even when you are thinking, the little voice inside of you is the one that composes that thought in your head). This is the key to manifestation: Use your feelings to ask for what you want. The Universe responds to what you are. And if you are happy (feeling happy), it will bring you more happiness. If you are abundant (feeling abundant), it will bring you more abundance. If you are healthy (feeling healthy), it will bring you more health, etc.

This is probably why, most of the time, you don't get what you truly desire; you say you want a certain thing or event to happen in your life, but you are really feeling the lack of it. You really feel that you don't have what you desire or dream about right now. You feel the opposite of what this desire will make you feel.

The Energy of the Universe doesn't understand words; it only understands energy—your feelings, your emotions. This is why you must feel and act as if what you desire is already present in your reality. Have you ever gotten that job where you nailed that interview? Have you gotten that first kiss you dreamed about over and over again? Guess what? You felt it before it happened. You not only mentally rehearsed getting that job or getting that first kiss, but you felt the feelings as if that experience had already happened, and guess what, it happened.

Feelings are the secret to this whole manifestation thing. You and I were never taught how to communicate through feelings; if anything, we were told to hide them. Society has created limiting beliefs around how boys and girls should behave. But when it comes to your dreams and your desires, you must throw this out of the window. These limiting beliefs were created by a limited mind; they don't serve you. You must learn how to communicate with Energy Source through your feelings. Learn how to talk feelings.

There is one more thing I would like you to pay attention to. You don't really desire what you think you desire. Let me explain this a little further. What you are truly after, what you truly desire, are the feelings you would experience after getting what you desire. You don't want to win the lottery; you want to feel freedom. Feel free, and you will experience more freedom. You don't want to overcome an addiction; you want to feel healthy. Feel healthy, and you will experience more health in your life. You don't want a boyfriend or a girlfriend; you want to feel love. Feel love for yourself, and love will come into your life, etc.

When *asking* and *communicating* with the Universe, communicate through feelings. Understand that what you truly want is to feel happiness, love, peace, joy abundance, freedom, health, wealth, etc. Let the Universe give you the best outcome of what you are after. Detach yourself from the outcome, and you will receive miracles. Leave the "how" to the Divine Intelligence, and just learn how to talk feelings.

The Magic of Closing Your Eyes

There is something incredible that happens when you close your eyes. There is magic that happens when you go into the Invisible World. In the beginning, you might not like closing your eyes because you might not be used to doing so. You might have created the habit of not being able to close your eyes and focus your inner voice into the right conversation for more than five minutes. But the more you practice doing it, the better you will get at it; you will make this a habit. Closing your eyes is one of the most powerful tools you have to reconnect with Divine Energy. I can promise that once you start getting better at it, closing your eyes will be your go-to happy place.

When I started to close my eyes, in the beginning, I didn't really know what to do. I really didn't know what to think about. Here's one of the many things you can do when closing your eyes. Eventually, you will start to find your own way, but in the beginning, it's OK to look for inspiration on what to do.

This is a three-part meditation. It will take time to get through the whole thing, but it is totally worth it. You should allow yourself about 20–35 minutes to go through the whole thing. In the beginning, it might seem hard to get through it, but as with everything, the more you do this, the better you will get at it. These exercises are all meant to help you create the habit of living in your natural state of being—happiness, love, peace, and joy.

Part 1

Start by closing your eyes. Notice where your attention goes. Whenever your attention decides to escape to any thought (positive or negative), bring it back to this present moment by saying, "I am here; I am now." The second your mind starts to wander, become aware of what is happening, and bring your attention back into this present moment. Wherever they might be, bring your thoughts back into the black screen behind your eyes.

Start practicing this for about five minutes. In the beginning, this is going to be very hard. You might need to bring your attention back into the present moment every five seconds; this is normal. Remember, your attention is like a little puppy-dog who wants to go everywhere, play with everything, and do anything, but you have to train it to sit still. It's only when you acknowledge that your attention is loose that you can start gaining control over it.

For the next five to ten minutes, every time your attention goes somewhere else that is not *the present moment*, you have to bring it back to *now*. I promise you will get better at this. This is how you recover the ability to instruct yourself what to think and what to feel, no matter what might be happening in your outer environment. This is how you start creating the *habit of magic*. After practicing this for a few days, you can now move to Part 2.

Part 2

After Part 1, continue to keep your eyes closed; you are about to have an honest conversation with yourself. Don't worry, no one is listening, and there are no judgments. This is between you and you alone. Remember, you must be honest with yourself.

Bring your awareness to the limiting beliefs or negative emotions that you constantly think you have. You may want to think about these negative emotions first before you close your eyes. You might want to grab a piece of paper and write down at least five negative thoughts or emotions that you keep telling yourself. Memorize them so that you can then know what to *think about* once your eyes are closed.

What negative emotion do you feel most of the time? Is it fear, anger, hatred, anxiety, stress, loneliness, sadness? It's OK if you choose more than one. This exercise is meant to recognize those feelings so that you can then do something about them. A good thing to do is to focus on one or two per week. Work on one for a while, and whenever you start to feel better about it (and you will), you can move on to the next one.

So, let's speak about fear, for example. Fear could be present in many ways in your life; maybe you feel like you want to control things in your life because you are afraid of the unknown. Maybe fear comes into your life in the form of lack and scarcity; you might feel there is not enough money, time, or energy in the day. Fear might be present in your life when you feel unworthy, or you might feel like there might be something *wrong* with you (which is not true; I can promise you, you are perfect).

Normally, negative emotions are all linked together. So don't worry; just pick one, and work on it. For example, fear can lead to anger, anger to anxiety, stress, hatred, and so on. Fear is one of the largest negative emotions that connects all of them. Fear might be a good place to start.

Once you pick the negative emotions that you are going to work on, you can move on to the second part of the exercise.

Imagine *pushing* these negative emotions outside of you. Imagine that you are literally pushing a giant black ball of energy (the negative emotion) that's coming from within. Once this black energy ball exists outside of you, throw it away as hard and as far as you can. As you are throwing it away, you can say something like, "This feeling of *fear* (for example) doesn't serve me anymore. I don't need this in my life anymore. I let it go." Go to the next feeling and do the same thing.

After you're done with the two to five feelings you are working on, imagine that you place them inside a box. Once they exist inside of this box, imagine putting a lock on this box. You are now going to imagine that you give this box away to the Divine Energy, an energy that has no limits and can do it all. Ask this Divine Energy to take these negative emotions and transform them into something beautiful. Ask this Divine Intelligence to give this energy back to you whenever it is ready and pure; because, remember, negative feelings are energy as well. You are asking this Divine Intelligence to transform this negative energy into something beautiful, and you trust that you will get it back in the form of Pure Love Force. Lastly, imagine seeing this box disappearing into the blackness of nowhere; allow yourself to feel that these feelings are no longer inside of you.

Now we can move to Part 3.

Part 3

After finishing Part 2 of this meditation, you are now a clean slate, an empty canvas. You've just gotten rid of the feelings and emotions that no longer serve you. Now the fun part begins.

Imagine the best version of yourself. What does the best version of you look like? What are the feelings related to this version of yourself? It is also a good idea to write down all the qualities that you know this best version of yourself possesses. This time, write as much as you can. Who is this incredible person? You can write things like: "I am love, I am grateful, I am beautiful, I am greatness, I am abundant, I am powerful, I am healthy, I am wealthy, I am courageous, I am creative, I am unlimited, I am rich, I am freedom, I am incredible, I am a genius, everything works out for me, I am in love with life," and so on. Write as much as you would like. Create this perfect version of you who lives the life you are meant to live.

Once you have a clear vision of the best you, you are going to focus your awareness on your heart. Your heart is the biggest energy centre in your entire body, and it is the source of your creative energy. Once you have clear focus on your heart, you are going to imagine a big source of light and heat coming from inside of your chest area; feel this energy inside of you. Feel how it becomes bigger and bigger, brighter and brighter, stronger and stronger. It is very important to feel it. Use your awareness and your imagination. Open your awareness. Open your heart.

The following is the most important part of this whole meditation.

Start feeling what love feels like. Start to train the cells in your body to simply feel love. Really get into feeling the emotion of love. Concentrate. Focus. Give it time. Try again. And again. And again. Do this for a couple of minutes. Then move on to the next feeling on your list. Spend a couple of minutes on this new feeling, then move on to the next. You are going to do this with at least five to ten of the emotions you wrote on your list. This is the most important part of the whole meditation. It is a good idea to give yourself about 20–25 minutes for this section. This part is the most important part of them all. You are creating new habits; you are recognizing who you truly are.

This is how you start living your dream life, by being this person today, in your meditations. If you train your body to feel the emotions of your future, you will start to live your future today. This is how you create a habit. This is how you live your dream life today. Eventually, everything around you will transform into your dream life. It will look like magic. It will seem like everything in your life starts to change all of a sudden. You will experience serendipitous moments; you will experience happy coincidences. Miracles will meet you. You cannot be two different people at once; eventually, you will be that powerful version you are imagining. You will start to live life from that best version of you; and it all started with a thought and a feeling—this is real magic.

Understanding the Magic of You

There's a lot of magic within you. I understand if you have some doubts about your innate ability to create and experience what you desire in this life; I had my own too. At first, I couldn't understand this concept of being able to create miracles in my life, this concept of being a creator. I had always thought that life is something that just happens to people. Now I see life as the gift to create whatever I decide; I am in control. I hope that with what you've been reading in this book, I've been able to help you understand that your internal dialogue, your identity, and your beliefs, believe it or not, are just habits you created over the years. These habits are running your life without you even noticing it. And you can change all of these to better serve you. You can choose to create other habits—magical habits.

In the beginning, while you start practicing all of the material you are finding in this book, your old self, your fears, your old bad habits–your ego–will try to convince you that what you are now doing is a waste of your time. They will try to convince you that it is hard and that maybe you shouldn't do it, and perhaps it is not worth it. You are already living an OK life, so why bother?

These bad habits will become harder to overcome at first, as you are now shining light on them. You are breaking the addiction you have had for years of feeling a certain way. In this case, this is the storm before the calm. For the first time, in a very long time, you are now choosing to have pure, loving thoughts toward yourself. So, these ego habits of the past will create noise to try and distract you from overcoming them. They will try to make you feel more fear, more anxiety, more stress, and more sadness. And when this happens, you must go back to closing your eyes and remembering the best version of you that you are now *being and building upon.*

Remember that the words, "I am…", are the most powerful words you can ever speak or think. So, take a moment, take a deep breath, and re-center. "I am unlimited. I am love. I am abundance. I am freedom. I am powerful. I am happy. I am unstoppable…"

Throughout our lives, we have parents and teachers, and hopefully we also have mentors, people who teach us what they know about life. They try to give you and me the best tools for success that they *know,* but this is all based on their understanding and awareness of the world. Perhaps something new, which no one ever told you, was that after a few years, after you graduated college or university in around your late 20s, after becoming a full-grown adult, you were going to have to become your own teacher—your own parent. No one ever told you that after you left your parents' home, you were going to have to become your own parent.

No one told you that you would have to make yourself eat the vegetables you don't like eating. You would have to make yourself read the books you feel lazy to read. You would have to make yourself exercise when you don't want to. You would have to make yourself learn the habits of truly achieving inner peace, happiness, and joy. You would have to learn to choose the right thoughts, the right feelings, and the right actions. No one ever told you that the *real school* was just about to begin. No one ever told you that the biggest and hardest research paper you were ever going to have to *write*, is the one that answers the questions, "Who am I?" and "Why am I here?"

As you're learning to use your attention, your energy, and your awareness, please be patient with yourself.

Imagine a little baby girl as she is learning how to walk. In the very beginning, she is going to fall very frequently and constantly. And even though this little girl keeps failing at walking, and she is constantly falling on her back, you would never look at her baby face and say: "You dumb and stupid baby! Can't you see how easy it is to walk? Can't you see me walking! Just put one leg in front of the other without falling! Come on!"

You would never say these words. You don't even feel these emotions at all. When you see a baby learning how to walk, on the contrary, you are very caring, loving, patient, and understanding. You are excited at how this little creature is taking a monumental step in her life.

I would love for you to imagine that you are this little baby learning how to walk. You are now learning how to use your energy in a way that you have never used it before. You are developing these new muscles. Be as loving, patient, caring, and understanding as you would with a baby who is learning how to walk. Yes, there will be plenty of times that you will fall back on your butt, but that doesn't mean you will not learn how to *properly walk*. You will *walk*, and one day, you are going to *run*.

Are you a good parent to yourself? Are you a good teacher to yourself? Are you a good mentor to yourself? Are you being patient, loving, and caring toward yourself?

Chapter 10

Real Magic

Magic Revealed

"Peace cannot be kept by force;
it can only be achieved by understanding."
– Albert Einstein

There is a saying in magic that a magician never reveals his secrets. When it comes to *sleight of hand,* the ability of using my hands to create the illusion of magic, I don't want to reveal the method I use to accomplish any trick. If I were to tell you what I did to create the illusion of magic, you wouldn't feel wonder and astonishment anymore. It would take away the gift of this little miracle. It would take away the feeling that something impossible just became possible.

I came to the conclusion that the opposite is true when talking about *sleight of mind,* the ability of using my thoughts and feelings to create *real magic* in my life. I am going to reveal the secrets I use to create real magic in my life. I hope that this book has provided you with a guide to a deeper understanding of who you truly are, what you're capable of, and what you're truly meant to experience in this physical form. I hope that this book has helped you be aware that there is so much abundance in this Universe. I hope you truly feel that you are worthy of living and experiencing love, happiness, peace, and joy—this is your natural state of being.

I hope you understand and are familiarized with the idea that everything in this Physical Universe is energy. You can only create a change in your outside world by creating a change in your inside world. You can start creating changes by placing your awareness on the power that is living within you—the Divine Intelligence that exists in all things—and if you pay attention to the power within, you will attract more of the same.

This is my greatest magic trick; and with all my love, I'm revealing it to you. This might work for you; this might not. This is meant to be a guide for you to find your own way. This is meant to be a projection of your inner self deciding what it is that you want to try. Listen to your inner voice; it's designed to find your inner peace. It is designed to get you to enlightenment. Look at the following as a guide. I recognize that I don't have all the answers, and I am still playing with how to make *my magic* better. I recognize that I only know a small grain of sand in the entire beach. So, by all means, go find what works for you.

What you are about to read is very powerful, and if you can see and understand why it works, nothing, really nothing, will stop you from creating magic in your life. This will take time to build up to. It will take exploration. It will take practice. It will take love and patience. But you will get better, and most importantly, you will find not only what works for you and what doesn't, but you will find yourself. I still remember how I didn't know where to start. I didn't know what to do. It took me about three months to be able to sit through the whole thing. At the beginning, I could only do this for five minutes. After a week, I could do it for 10 minutes, then 15, and so on. Be patient, loving, kind, and caring with yourself, just as you are patient, caring, and loving when a baby is learning how to walk. You are learning how to walk again.

Once you find your own way into all of this, with time, you will change—you will evolve. It is meant to change; it is meant to evolve. Nothing stays the same. You will find answers in the form of ideas; you will think about new things to try, and ideas will come to you—try them. Discover yourself. Be playful with all of the ideas and concepts that connect you back to your Divine Energy Source. This is what we came here to do—to play.

The Reveal

Here is the secret to it all. It is broken into two parts. Be patient with yourself while practicing all of this. It will take some time to get this practice to where you want to get it. But I promise you one thing, you will find love, happiness, peace, joy, and so much more.

Part 1

In a "regular" work-week routine, you might have to get up around 7am to be at work by 8:45am. Let's say you work from 9am–6pm. Hopefully, you are back at home around 7pm. By the time you finish cooking and eating dinner, it is now 8:30pm. By the time you are peacefully sitting on your couch or your bed, it is now 9pm. It's only until about 9pm when you probably have the time to try and do something for yourself. You have about 2 to 2.5 hours to do something you would like to do for yourself before going to bed. But because it's the end of the day and you're tired, you end up watching TV, or scrolling through your social media like a zombie. And why wouldn't you? You're exhausted! You have already given so much of your energy away to your outer world (work and loved ones). But did you give your inner world (where change happens) any of that time, love, and energy?

You are full of dreams and goals you would like to achieve and/or experience. There are activities and ideas that inspire you and that you would like to do more of. But by the time you are able to get to any of these activities, your brain and body are exhausted; there is no more *juice* left. So you end up spending the last two-and-a-half to three hours of the day lying on the couch like a deflated balloon; or at least that is what was happening to me. So, here is where the secret to *Part 1* of the magic gets revealed.

You must take the last two to three hours of your day (9– 11:45pm) and shift that time over into your morning. This literally means you have to take those hours and take them out of your night and plug them into your morning.

For example, if you are waking up at 7:30am to be at work by 9am, you now must create the habit of waking up and being out of bed by 4:30am. I know this sounds crazy; I know it sounds impossible. You are probably thinking: "How dare you suggest that I get out of my cozy, fluffy bed at 4:30am!" Well, how bad do you want things in your life to change? I knew I wanted change very badly.

There is way more than meets the eye when you do this. There are two incredible magical things happening when you do this.

From a scientific point of view, there are two points during the day that your brain is the most susceptible to be reprogramed. One is very early in the morning, from 3:30am–5am, and the other one is at night before you go to sleep, just before you fall into complete sleep, when your body is fully asleep but your mind is still working. This is why it is so important to do this early in the morning.

You want to plant a new program and a new set of habits into your subconscious mind. From 3–5 am, your subconscious mind is the most susceptive. It is in a hypnotic state, where it is easier to change old habits and create new ones.

There is something extremely powerful about starting the day by doing something just for you and for nobody else. This is extremely empowering. Give yourself the gift of the first three hours of the day, from 4–7am. Spend that time focusing your thoughts and feelings (meditating), and doing something you love, such as painting, dancing, running, exercising, or reading— something that's just for you. When you do this, you are creating a new reality for yourself. You are pouring miracles into your life.

You won't see this in the very beginning, but the more you do this, the more powerful momentum you will create; and eventually, everything around you will start to change. Things will change because of you. And the best part is that if you give yourself these first few hours of the day, you can now be at peace with going out into the world and giving your time to others (work, family, and your must-do's). You will be happier to do so, because you've already accomplished so much for yourself.

I cannot stress this point enough. This is how miracles start to happen; this is where they start to happen. By you paying attention to yourself, by giving yourself love and energy, more of the same will come into your life. More energy and love will come into your life. Please try it. You are worth it. Trust and live in the unknown. You can start doing this by small increments of time. Try 30-minute increments each week until you get to your goal of 2.5 to 3 hours just for you.

Part 2

This is Part 2 of the secret to my magic, which also comes in a two-part experience.

This first part is to focus your thoughts and feelings with your eyes closed—meditation. This goes hand in hand with waking up at the time you read earlier in this chapter. As I mentioned before, this will also take practice and concentration. It will take time to build up to memorizing what to do. It will take practice to find your own way at it. But here is what to do once you close your eyes and sit still.

Remember, it is very important to honour that this is your time. This time is meant for you and you alone. During this time, you cannot allow anything into your mind that belongs to your outer life: your work, your family, other people, your ego, the things you *have to do* during the day, debt, health problems, or your overall problems, whatever they might be. Whenever you go inside, you have to make the commitment that the person who is going to stand up after this time with yourself, is not going to be the same person that sat down. This is your time and no one else's. You will come out of your meditation as a butterfly.

This meditation practice is a personal practice. This is something that you should keep personal. This is between you and you only. The more you keep this private to yourself, the more it gains momentum; after all, your dreams are yours.

If you want to know what I personally do in my meditation, please go to my website, **sleightofmindbook.com,** where you can find a step-by-step guide on what to do.

The second part of this *Part 2* is to do something that inspires you. That's it. This is simple yet powerful. Perhaps you love writing poems, or maybe you love painting, or going for a run, or dancing, singing, playing an instrument, or working on that side project you've been thinking about. This last 45 minutes to an hour, you need to work or create something tangible for yourself. Create a possibility. Send that email you've always wanted to and never dared to. Start that online business idea that has been tucked away inside your head. Maybe you don't necessarily know where to start. Just play around with ideas, and write them down; it is all part of the process. Perhaps you start writing a book and title it *Sleight of Mind* (see what I did there?).

What you do with this time is up to you. The only two rules are to do something that inspires you (something that connects with your Divine Energy), and to do something just for you and nobody else. I hope you understand the power of this. I hope you can see the power in the magic I just revealed to you. This time is a gift to yourself so that you can create your new life. This is the time to reconnect with the Energy Source that creates worlds, so that you can create your new world. Building this habit will take patience and love. But after a while, you will be unstoppable. You will be a miracle magnet, and you will be everything you have ever wanted to be. As a matter of fact, you already are all of those things; you just have to re-discover them.

The Show Must Go On

This is a summary of the principles and concepts in this book. This is what I've learned so far, and apply every day, using *Sleight of Mind*. This is what I hope would be a guide for you to open your heart and your mind to creating your own magic in your own way. All I ask is for you to be open to the new concepts that you have read in this book. The fact that you are reading the messages written in this book, is not an accident; there are no accidents. It is no accident that you and I have crossed paths in this life. Or perhaps you ended up with this book in your hands in a very unique and wonderful way. What matters is that the Universe is always saying "yes"; it is always speaking to you. The language of miracles is always being spoken. The question is, are you listening, and are you paying attention?

It is my greatest hope that what's in this book might lead you to *that* thought, which might lead you to *that* thing, which might lead you to *that* other thought, which might lead you to *that* other thing, which… (you get the idea). Give yourself all the credit, as you are now fully aware that you are the creator of your own reality. Run your own show, create your own magic, and experience miracles in your life.

1. The real you & the world within

Recognize that you are more than meets the physical eye. Recognize that you are way more than the ideas, thoughts, and beliefs that were passed on to you. Recognize that there is an invisible part of you, a reflection of the Universe. Recognize that you are part of the Divine Energy. You are not a body that has a spirit inside, but you are a spirit that has a body inside.

You came from the same energy that created everything; therefore, you can also create anything and everything. Be humble to the idea that we are all the same, and that we are all part of one whole collective consciousness that wants life to exist. Your natural state of being is happiness, love, peace, and joy. Recognize the fact that there is something inside of you that is connected to everything. You are unlimited, you are almighty, you are a creator, and you are here for a reason. Recognize your power within. You are Divine by nature.

Remember who you truly are. You are not your name, your age, your gender, your ethnicity, your identity, or your personality. You are a Spiritual Energy Being having a human experience. Go have fun creating.

2. Energy is all there is

Everything in this Universe is made out of energy. The smallest particles inside of an atom are energy. Emotions are energy in motion. Thoughts are energy. Energy is all there is. Use this understanding to adopt a life where you stop trying to change matter with matter, and start changing matter (your physical world) with energy (the Spiritual World and the World Inside of you). Remember, energy can never be created or destroyed; it can only be transformed.

Change your energy, change your life.

3. Your thoughts & feelings

There is an eternal thinking and feeling loop. No matter where you get into this loop, either through a thought or through a feeling, be conscious of all your thoughts and all your feelings, all day, every day. Frequently ask yourself: "What am I thinking about right now? How am I feeling? Are these thoughts or feelings aligned with what I truly desire in my life?" You must always be playing this never-ending game of monitoring your thoughts and feelings.

Thoughts become things. Don't think of what you want; think **from** what you want. Imagine living your life from the time and space of your wishes fulfilled. Express only the feelings related to your wishes as if they had already happened.

Speak to the Universe through feelings. Feelings are the language of the Universe, not words.

4. Habits

You and I are habitual creatures. Remember, everything about you is a habit that is being run by your subconscious program.

Be aware of your habits—are they good or are they bad?

Constantly ask yourself: "Am I living in survival mode or in creative mode?" Whenever you feel stressed, anxious, or angry, be patient with yourself, and remind yourself that these feelings are just habits you are trying to get rid of. Try connecting with your creative mode more often. Live inspired.

Make a conscious effort to teach your body the habit of feeling love, happiness, peace, and joy. Make a habit of feeling these every day during a private time where you can focus your thoughts and feelings to practice how they feel.

Practice over and over again the best version of yourself. Sit down and write on a piece of paper the best version of you; then mentally rehearse it every day. Ask the questions: "How does this best version of me behave and feel? What does he/she do? How does he/she react to work? What does he/she do for a living, pleasure, vacations, eating? How does he/she think, feel, and act?" Don't leave out any details. Practice being this person right now, over and over again.

5. *Always choose now*

Life is an eternal present moment. There is no past; there is no future. Time is just an illusion created by a limited mind to give *structure* to things and to control something that is really eternal.

Keep bringing your attention into this present moment as often as you can. Everything that has ever happened to you is not here anymore; you must let go of what you cannot grab. It is only in the now that you can make a change to your life. Stop giving your energy away to any of the thoughts of your past, or to the thoughts of a future based on your past. If you are truly committed to changing your life, it has to be in the now. You need that energy that you keep giving away to your past and future; you need that energy in the present moment.

Remember, when you are in the now, you are not your name, your age, gender, ethnicity, identity, beliefs, personality, etc. When you are in the now, you simply are. When you are in the now, you are anything and everything you desire to be; there is no past and no future, only the decision you make.

"Wisdom is knowing I am nothing. Love is knowing I am everything, and between the two my life moves."
— **Nisargadatta Maharaj**

6. Silence & meditation

Everything was created from silence. There is a lot of noise out there dividing your attention and your energy. Have a daily practice of silence. In silence, you will find peace. In silence, you will find the answers. Silence is key to everything, yet most people are afraid to stop and do nothing. Start contemplating nature; start closing your eyes and listening to nothingness. Before anything was created, there was silence.

Meditation is focus thinking. Have a daily practice where you can focus your thoughts and regain control of your thoughts and feelings. Go into that Invisible World where you can start creating anything you desire. Love, happiness, peace, and joy are always waiting for you to take a moment and connect to them. Meditation is truly just a form of connecting to that Divine Intelligence that is always there for you, to remind you of who you truly are—a powerful Divine creator.

7. Imagination

> **"You were not given the power of imagination without also being given the power of creation."**
> **– Wayne Dyer**

This is a very powerful phrase I carry with me all the time. Mentally rehearsing and picturing your dream life is the key to experiencing it. Can you use your imagination to think *from* what you want, and live your current life as though your desires had already happened? Use your imagination not to think of what you want, but to think *from* what you want. Have fun with every single detail. The sky is not the limit. You are unlimited.

With your imagination, you are taking the smallest particles of energy that exist within your desires, and you are transforming them from waves into particles; this is a principle of quantum physics. The longer you imagine and live *from* those thoughts, the more energy you collapse into matter. Use your imagination, and let your desired experiences come to you. Never let go of your dreams; put them in the middle of your heart and your mind, and always imagine them as your reality.

Go into that Invisible World and start pulling that dream life into your Visible World. Imagination is key to man's reality.

Imagination is pure consciousness in action; it is true Divine Power.

8. Gratitude

Everyone has so much to be grateful for. Don't take anything for granted; there is so much to be grateful for. Just start being grateful for the *simple* things your body can do, like breathing, smiling, eating, seeing, listening, walking, etc. Then, continue with everything that's around you, like love, peace, happiness, nature, other people, etc. Never take for granted the fact that you can smile at another human being. Never take for granted the fact that you can be kind to others. The more you are grateful for, the more you will receive. I once heard someone say:

"Gratitude is the only *rent* we need to pay while being alive on this planet."

Gratitude is the most powerful vibration there is. You are always thankful once something has been given to you. So, are you able to be grateful for something that has not yet happened? By being grateful, you are teaching your body and cells that whatever you are grateful for, has already happened.

9. Keep on playing

Remind yourself every day to live your life in childlike wonder. Go back to that mentality of experiencing the world in awe and excitement. Go back and remember what it was like to play. Dance, sing, paint, run, do arts and crafts, travel, pick up a hobby or two, play an instrument, learn something new, etc. Play again; it's the only way you will be in touch with what truly inspires you. Never stop playing. It's one of the only things we came into this world to do.

10. *Speaking miracles and seeing magic*

Every day and every second carries a miracle that's speaking to you, from that cloud formation that you'll never see again in the sky, to your amazing human body that operates by itself and repairs itself, to that traffic jam, to the rain, and to all this life has to offer. Experiencing magic, and speaking the language of miracles, is something you simply tune into. It is always there, but sometimes we are the ones who choose not to pay attention to all the love and the miracles that exist in front of us.

The more magic and miracles you pay attention to, the more magic and miracles you will create in your own personal life. Creating and experiencing magic is a habit. Miracles are a habit. First you need to be open to see them, and it is only then that you will understand how to create them. I truly believe we are experiencing *heaven on earth*. Right now, you have the consciousness and awareness to enjoy tasty food, laugh, smile, be happy, walk, talk to someone, drink a sip of water, see the sky, see a sunrise, tell someone "I love you," etc.; you have the gift of experiencing all of these and more. These are real miracles; these are the small things that build up to the big miracles.

11. *Love is all there is*

Love is all there is; everything else is an illusion. All those negative feelings are just illusions that come from the separation you have created from the only truth that exists—love is all there is.

You are a piece of this Universe, and you are a part of this Divine Energy; therefore, you have the same abilities as the energy you came from. You came from this Divine Love that creates life and keeps everything in perfect harmony; you can do all of the same.

Everything in this life carries a message of love. Everything is love. Sometimes it might be really hard to see love in what happens around us, but I can promise you that everything that is happening for you is because of love. And when you realize that no one is after you, and that life is happening for you, you will start to see true love in things. We are all one with everything and everyone. We all come from the same place—Divine Energy. The key to everything in this life is unconditional love.

We are all in this world together. We are all one. Even when someone might not act like it, just remember that there are old habits they are trying to break.

Love is patient and kind. Always act from love. Love all, but most importantly, love yourself. Love can move mountains; love transforms. Make a conscious effort to always do everything with love—the way you respond, the way you react, the way you say things, the way you do things, etc.

"You are either a host to love, or a hostage to your ego."
– Wayne Dyer

12. Live in-spirit

Live inspired. Seek to do activities and think the thoughts that inspire you. No matter where you are, seek inspiration. Dance, sing, run, cook, paint, write, play, perform, draw, exercise, etc. Do more of what you love. This world needs more people connected to their spirit. Live life connected to your creative power. This is the key to your power. Live inspired; live in-spirit.

Now You See Me, Now You...

Thank you for being open to the words inside this book. Thank you for embracing the invisible part of you that is connected to everything. Thank you for being you.

You are perfect. You are magic. You are a miracle. You are love. You are whole. You are unlimited. You have the power that creates worlds inside of you. You are pure Divine Love Energy, capable of creating anything and everything.

This is your life, your reality, your moment. Don't wait for something to happen to do the things you love or to be the *YOU* that you desire to be. There is unlimited potential inside of you, waiting for you to pay attention to it. Play, run, sing, do, try, smile, eat, laugh, love—do anything and everything. Listen to your inside. Be at peace with what is. Everything you desire is already in this physical world, waiting for you to pay attention to it. Create your own magic; experience the miracles you desire right now with your imagination first. Use love as your language.

I want to leave you with this last quote from a great teacher, a quote that can bring you that power and spirit every time you read it. Remember, the best magic there is, is the magic of being your true self. This world needs more of you.

> *"Don't die with your music still in you."*
> – **Wayne Dyer**

About the Author

Rodrigo Diaz lives in Toronto, Canada.

The author is available for delivering keynote presentations, attending speaking events, and providing personal consulting, lectures, seminars, and one-on-one coaching to appropriate audiences (big and small) around the world. Help Rodrigo Diaz spread this message of empowerment and understanding to everyone around you. For rates and availability, please contact the author directly at:

rodrigodiazmercado@gmail.com

To order more books, please contact the author directly, or please visit:

sleightofmindbook.com

Finally, if you have been inspired by this book, the best thing you could ever do is pass it on and be a wonderful role model for others. This world needs more magic; this world needs more of your magic.

9 7 8 1 7 7 2 7 7 3 1 2 5